Forensic Science:
Evidence, Clues, and Investigation

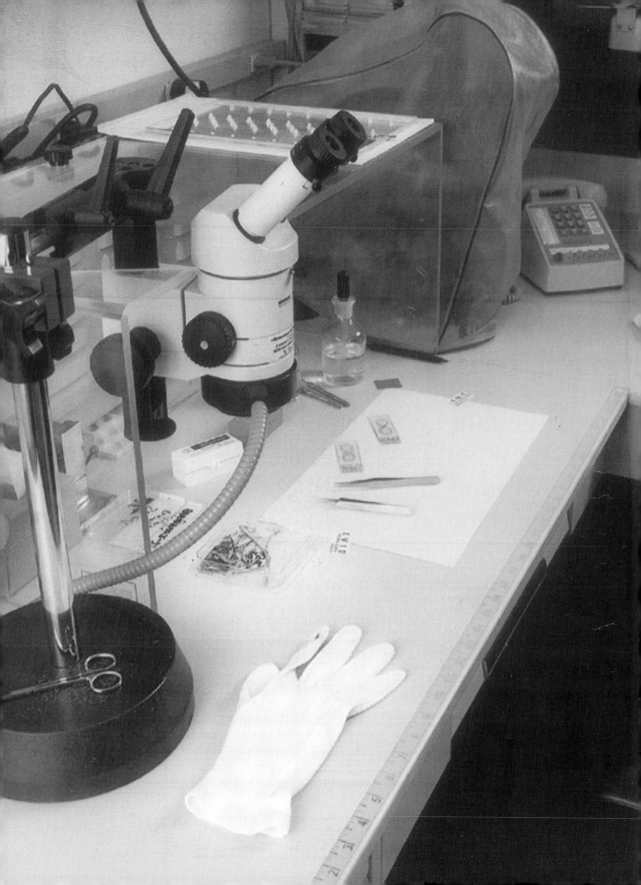

CRIME, JUSTICE, AND PUNISHMENT

Forensic Science:
Evidence, Clues, and Investigation

Gregory Middle School
2621 Springdale Circle
Naperville, Illinois 60565

Andrea Campbell

Austin Sarat, GENERAL EDITOR

CHELSEA HOUSE PUBLISHERS
Philadelphia

Frontis: *Tools for forensic hair analysis.*

Cover Photo Skull: PhotoDisc
Background Series 5, BS05014
All other photos: courtesy the FBI

Chelsea House Publishers

Editor in Chief Stephen Reginald
Managing Editor James D. Gallagher
Production Manager Pamela Loos
Art Director Sara Davis
Director of Photography Judy L. Hasday
Senior Production Editor Lisa Chippendale

Staff for FORENSIC SCIENCE

Senior Editor John Ziff
Associate Art Director/Designer Takeshi Takahashi
Picture Researcher Patricia Burns
Cover Illustrator Takeshi Takahashi

3 5 7 9 8 6 4

The Chelsea House World Wide Web site address is
http://www.chelseahouse.com

Library of Congress Cataloging-in-Publication Data

Campbell, Andrea.
Forensic science: evidence, clues, and investigation /
Andrea Campbell.
    p. 136 cm. — (Crime, justice, and punishment)
Includes bibliographical references and index.
Summary: Examines forensic science and how it can be
used to apprehend criminals by finding clues in rug fibers,
the way a bone is broken, DNA "fingerprints," and more.

ISBN 0-7910-4950-7

1. Forensic sciences—Juvenile literature. 2. Criminal
investigation—Juvenile literature. 3. Crime laboratories—
Juvenile literature. [1. Forensic sciences.
2. Criminal investigation.] I. Title. II. Series.
HV8073.C318 1999
363.25—dc21   99-19454
                                              CIP

Contents

CRIME, JUSTICE, AND PUNISHMENT

CAPITAL PUNISHMENT

CHILDREN, VIOLENCE, AND MURDER

CLASSIC CONS AND SWINDLES

CRIMES AGAINST CHILDREN:
CHILD ABUSE AND NEGLECT

CRIMES AGAINST HUMANITY

CYBER CRIMES

DETERRENCE AND REHABILITATION

DRUGS, CRIME,
AND CRIMINAL JUSTICE

THE DUTY TO RESCUE

ESPIONAGE AND TREASON

THE FBI'S MOST WANTED

FORENSIC SCIENCE

THE GRAND JURY

GREAT PROSECUTIONS

HATE CRIMES

HIGH CRIMES AND MISDEMEANORS:
THE IMPEACHMENT PROCESS

INFAMOUS TRIALS

THE INSANITY DEFENSE

JUDGES AND SENTENCING

THE JURY SYSTEM

JUVENILE CRIME

MAJOR UNSOLVED CRIMES

ORGANIZED CRIME

POLICE AND POLICING

PRISONS

PRIVATE INVESTIGATORS
AND BOUNTY HUNTERS

RACE, CRIME, AND PUNISHMENT

REVENGE AND RETRIBUTION

RIGHTS OF THE ACCUSED

SERIAL MURDER

TERRORISM

VICTIMS AND VICTIMS' RIGHTS

WHITE-COLLAR CRIME

Fears and Fascinations:

An Introduction to
Crime, Justice, and Punishment

By Austin Sarat

We live with crime and images of crime all around us. Crime evokes in most of us a deep aversion, a feeling of profound vulnerability, but it also evokes an equally deep fascination. Today, in major American cities the fear of crime is a major fact of life, some would say a disproportionate response to the realities of crime. Yet the fear of crime is real, palpable in the quickened steps and furtive glances of people walking down darkened streets. At the same time, we eagerly follow crime stories on television and in movies. We watch with a "who done it" curiosity, eager to see the illicit deed done, the investigation undertaken, the miscreant brought to justice and given his just deserts. On the streets the presence of crime is a reminder of our own vulnerability and the precariousness of our taken-for-granted rights and freedoms. On television and in the movies the crime story gives us a chance to probe our own darker motives, to ask "Is there a criminal within?" as well as to feel the collective satisfaction of seeing justice done.

Fear and fascination, these two poles of our engagement with crime, are, of course, only part of the story. Crime is, after all, a major social and legal problem, not just an issue of our individual psychology. Politicians today use our fear of, and fascination with, crime for political advantage. How we respond to crime, as well as to the political uses of the crime issue, tells us a lot about who we are as a people as well as what we value and what we tolerate. Is our response compassionate or severe? Do we seek to understand or to punish, to enact an angry vengeance or to rehabilitate and welcome the criminal back into our midst? The CRIME, JUSTICE, AND PUNISHMENT series is designed to explore these themes, to ask why we are fearful and fascinated, to probe the meanings and motivations of crimes and criminals and of our responses to them, and, finally, to ask what we can learn about ourselves and the society in which we live by examining our responses to crime.

Crime is always a challenge to the prevailing normative order and a test of the values and commitments of law-abiding people. It is sometimes a Raskolnikov-like act of defiance, an assertion of the unwillingness of some to live according to the rules of conduct laid out by organized society. In this sense, crime marks the limits of the law and reminds us of law's all-too-regular failures. Yet sometimes there is more desperation than defiance in criminal acts; sometimes they signal a deep pathology or need in the criminal. To confront crime is thus also to come face-to-face with the reality of social difference, of class privilege and extreme deprivation, of race and racism, of children neglected, abandoned, or abused whose response is to enact on others what they have experienced themselves. And occasionally crime, or what is labeled a criminal act, represents a call for justice, an appeal to a higher moral order against the inadequacies of existing law.

Figuring out the meaning of crime and the motivations of criminals and whether crime arises from defiance, desperation, or the appeal for justice is never an easy task. The motivations and meanings of crime are as varied as are the persons who engage in criminal conduct. They are as mysterious as any of the mysteries of the human soul. Yet the desire to know the secrets of crime and the criminal is a strong one, for in that knowledge may lie one step on the road to protection, if not an assurance of one's own personal safety. Nonetheless, as strong as that desire may be, there is no available technology that can allow us to know the whys of crime with much confidence, let alone a scientific certainty. We can, however, capture something about crime by studying the defiance, desperation, and quest for justice that may be associated with it. Books in the CRIME, JUSTICE, AND PUNISHMENT series will take up that challenge. They tell stories of crime and criminals, some famous, most not, some glamorous and exciting, most mundane and commonplace.

This series will, in addition, take a sober look at American criminal justice, at the procedures through which we investigate crimes and identify criminals, at the institutions in which innocence or guilt is determined. In these procedures and institutions we confront the thrill of the chase as well as the challenge of protecting the rights of those who defy our laws. It is through the efficiency and dedication of law enforcement that we might capture the criminal; it is in the rare instances of their corruption or brutality that we feel perhaps our deepest betrayal. Police, prosecutors, defense lawyers, judges, and jurors administer criminal justice and in their daily actions give substance to the guarantees of the Bill of Rights. What is an adversarial system of justice? How does it work? Why do we have it? Books in the CRIME, JUSTICE, AND PUNISHMENT series will examine the thrill of the chase as we seek to capture the criminal. They will also reveal the drama and majesty of the criminal trial as well as the day-to-day reality of a criminal justice system in which trials are the exception and negotiated pleas of guilty are the rule.

When the trial is over or the plea has been entered, when we have separated the innocent from the guilty, the moment of punishment has arrived. The injunction to punish the guilty, to respond to pain inflicted by inflicting pain, is as old as civilization itself. "An eye for an eye and a tooth for a tooth" is a biblical reminder that punishment must measure pain for pain. But our response to the criminal must be better than and different from the crime itself. The biblical admonition, along with the constitutional prohibition of "cruel and unusual punishment," signals that we seek to punish justly and to be just not only in the determination of who can and should be punished, but in how we punish as well. But neither reminder tells us what to do with the wrongdoer. Do we rape the rapist, or burn the home of the arsonist? Surely justice and decency say no. But, if not, then how can and should we punish? In a world in which punishment is neither identical to the crime nor an automatic response to it, choices must be made and we must make them. Books in the CRIME, JUSTICE, AND PUNISHMENT series will examine those choices and the practices, and politics, of punishment. How do we punish and why do we punish as we do? What can we learn about the rationality and appropriateness of today's responses to crime by examining our past and its responses? What works? Is there, and can there be, a just measure of pain?

CRIME, JUSTICE, AND PUNISHMENT brings together books on some of the great themes of human social life. The books in this series capture our fear and fascination with crime and examine our responses to it. They remind us of the deadly seriousness of these subjects. They bring together themes in law, literature, and popular culture to challenge us to think again, to think anew, about subjects that go to the heart of who we are and how we can and will live together.

*   *   *   *   *

Fighting crime is an extraordinarily complex activity. It requires a combination of patience, judgment, and increasingly a command of the complex technologies for decoding physical evidence. No crime is completely clean. Bodies leave marks, some microscopic, some more recognizable. These marks can be read by a skilled eye. As cases like the criminal trial of O. J. Simpson remind us, judgments of guilt or innocence often depend on the availability and interpretation of such evidence. Increasingly we turn to the scientific analysis of bodily traces, like DNA, to help solve crimes. Increasingly law depends on science.

Forensic Science provides a fascinating look at the various types of physical evidence as well as the various forensic techniques and technologies used in law enforcement. It tells its story through literature and film, but most of all through actual criminal cases. It shows us how the ingenuity of the detective is both supplemented and, to some extent, replaced by the precision of scientific analysis. In so doing it reminds us that the student of law needs to be familiar with a wide range of knowledge.

The book raises important questions about the future of law enforcement and its collaboration with science. Will the progress of forensic science outstrip our capacity to use it wisely? Or will we be able to use it to make more complete our quest for accuracy and fairness in the administration of criminal justice? These are questions of enormous importance, and they are wonderfully illuminated in *Forensic Science*.

HARD EVIDENCE

Sherlock Holmes began single-handedly solving the most baffling fictional crimes more than 100 years ago. His secret? Keen powers of observation, appreciation of the significance of seemingly minor clues, and rigorous logic. Today, criminal investigations are collaborative efforts and forensic science uses high-tech tools, but Holmes's method remains essentially unchanged.

To the police inspector, it seemed like an open-and-shut case: in the early hours of the morning, after a restless night spent pacing his bedroom and smoking, the dead man, Mr. Blessington, had hanged himself.

Carefully analyzing the crime scene, however, the detective came to a different conclusion: it was a clear case of murder. The police had discovered crucial evidence—four cigar stubs in the fireplace and ashes in several places around the room—but they failed to recognize its importance. When he examined the dead man's cigar case, the detective, whose expertise extended to cigars and even to ash, quickly realized that Blessington had not been smoking the night before he died. His cigars were Havanas, whereas the stubs in the fireplace were from the Dutch East Indies. Moreover, two of the cigar ends had been cut off with a blunt knife, and two had been bitten off by a set of excellent teeth. That meant that two men besides the deceased had been present in the bedroom, and other evidence pointed to the presence of a third man who had not smoked. To the amazement of the police inspector, the detective reconstructed the details of the murder, all "deduced from signs so subtle and minute" that the policeman could barely follow his reasoning.

The inspector should not have been amazed. After all, the detective had spent a lifetime honing his skills of observation and his knowledge of various sciences. He could tell which part of the city a man had been in from the mud on the man's pants. He could recite details about the life of a person he had just met simply by carefully observing the person's appearance and demeanor.

The detective in question was arguably the greatest crime investigator in history. He was also purely fictional, a creation of the British author Sir Arthur Conan Doyle. His name, of course, is Sherlock Holmes.

Holmes, who first appeared in 1887 in the novel *A Study in Scarlet*, was years ahead of his time. He understood that small and apparently insignificant clues—evidence the police investigators of his day routinely overlooked—often hold the key to understanding a case. His exceptional powers of observation and analysis, combined with his extensive knowledge of various sciences, enabled him to single-handedly solve the most baffling crimes.

Today, more than a century after Sherlock Holmes first astonished and delighted readers with his brilliance, most crimes are still solved the way they were in the Victorian era: through confessions or eyewitness accounts. Increasingly, however, police and prosecutors rely on evidence of the type Holmes often used to get at the truth: scientific, or forensic, evidence. Today that evidence typically comes from sources such as fingerprints, body fluids, and bullets.

In contrast to the romantic image of one Holmes-like supersleuth single-handedly uncovering the facts of a case, truth seeking in law enforcement and criminal justice is actually a collaborative effort, involving the police, a medical examiner or coroner, investigators, and lab technicians. Each applies his or her own expertise to the problem. But modern criminal investigations still begin in a manner Sherlock Holmes would find familiar—with careful examination of the crime scene. After police have secured the site, criminal investigators collect physical evidence. This evidence will be sent to crime labs, where expert technicians and forensic scientists will analyze it. Their findings, in turn, will affect the course of the police investigation and, if a suspect is charged, will be presented to the jury at trial.

In our title, we have referred rather informally to forensic science. However, distinction should be made between the terms *forensic science* and *criminalistics*, which are often used interchangeably. Forensic science is science applied to answering legal questions. It draws together principles and knowledge from one field, or a combination of fields—such as medicine, mathematics, physics, chemistry, biology, and anthropology—and applies them to legal proceedings. For example, *serology* is the study of blood and other body fluids; *forensic serology* is the study of blood and body-fluid evidence to help reconstruct a crime or an accident. Criminalistics, on the other hand, is a branch of forensic science that deals

Police tape cordons off the site of a homicide. Securing the crime scene, which may contain crucial forensic evidence, is the first step in a homicide investigation.

The arrangement of objects at a crime scene can provide important clues. Skilled police take pains not to disturb anything until the crime scene is analyzed and photographed.

specifically with the scientific collection and examination of physical evidence as it relates to a crime. Any references in this book to forensic science are actually references to the entire field of discovery.

But what exactly is forensic evidence? How is it used, and what does it mean in court?

Like any competitive game, a criminal trial is governed by rules. The rules of evidence dictate how evidence can be presented in the courtroom. For example, the prosecution, or the attorney representing the state (and the people in that state), may present various legal proofs in order to convince the judge or jury of the defendant's guilt. These can be witnesses, records, documents, objects, or other materials.

Four kinds of evidence may be admitted at trial:

1. *Testimony*, statements from competent, sworn witnesses.
2. *Direct evidence*, which refers to observations of eyewitnesses.

3. *Circumstantial evidence,* which is any information that tends to prove or disprove a point at issue.

4. *Real,* or *physical, evidence,* sometimes also called *hard evidence,* which refers to any tangible article or object of any kind, such as fingerprints, weapons, and bloodstains. (Real evidence may also include facsimiles such as photographs and reproductions.)

Seldom is guilt proved or blame assessed with a single piece of evidence. But forensic evidence, which falls into the fourth category above, often serves as the added weight that helps tip the scales of justice. It may be used to reconstruct the crime, identify participants, or confirm or discredit an alibi. It also frequently helps to eliminate suspects. It establishes the facts of the crime—for example, that the bullet that lodged in the victim's heart and caused his death came from the defendant's gun. It can provide a step-by-step analysis of the events leading up to, including, and following the incident. In short, forensic science can be the glue that holds all the facts of a case together.

Sometimes prosecutors have little except forensic evidence from which to construct a case; other times they use forensic evidence merely to corroborate the other types of evidence they've developed. Forensic evidence does not serve all cases. Typically it plays a far more important role in the investigation of violent crimes than in the investigation of property crimes or of accidents. But one thing is certain. Forensic evidence is static. It stands immobile. Because unless the criminal takes something away from the crime scene, hard evidence does not leave. Unlike witnesses, it will not change its mind or forget. Unlike crime scene bystanders, hard evidence will not get confused or become frightened. And unlike criminals, it will not make up stories or lie.

Yet hard evidence is only as reliable as the people who collect, analyze, and interpret it. At trial, different experts sometimes draw different conclusions from the same evidence. And defense attorneys frequently attack the validity of forensic evidence by pointing to lapses in the way the evidence was collected or handled. Thus it is essential that law enforcement officers, forensic scientists, and prosecutors understand and meticulously follow proper evidence-handling procedures. Otherwise the guilty may go free, or the innocent may be wrongly convicted.

For the forensic scientist, professional training and expertise, along with a healthy dose of intuition, are indispensable to the correct interpretation of evidence. Equally important is a questioning mind. For although you might not think about it in this way, forensic science begins as questions.

The initial inquiry can be defined as the "science of observation." It's an important element that goes a long

Forensic Evidence in the Criminal Justice Process

According to criminal justice researchers, police are on average about three times more likely to solve cases when scientific evidence is gathered and analyzed. In addition, when forensic evidence strongly associates a defendant with a crime, prosecutors are less likely to enter into plea negotiations, by which the defendant is offered the opportunity to plead guilty to a lesser charge in exchange for a more lenient sentence than he or she would receive if convicted at trial. And somewhat surprisingly, convicted defendants tend to receive more severe sentences if forensic evidence was presented at their trials. In fact, while controlling for a range of variables, researchers have found that forensic evidence is the only type of evidence that influences the severity of sanctions.

A nationwide survey of laboratory caseloads found that drugs and fingerprints made up from 60 to 80 percent of the evidence described in laboratory reports. Laboratory directors cite forensic evidence as having great importance in drug and homicide prosecutions, moderate importance in arsons and burglaries, and minimal importance in aggravated batteries, robberies, and larcenies. Lab directors also believe their examinations have substantial impact in rape cases. In general, scientific evidence has its greatest impact in cases where the chances of solution are smallest—when suspects are neither named nor identified quickly after the crime.

Information adapted from Joseph L. Peterson, *Use of Forensic Evidence by the Police in Court* (Washington, D.C.: U.S. Department of Justice, National Institute of Justice, 1987): 2, 3, 5.

way toward solving a crime or figuring out what happened to create a particular misfortune. To an expert like a seasoned police investigator, the scene of a crime or accident, which might include a body and associative evidence, provides significant information on which to base an investigation. Let's walk through the initial stages of a homicide investigation to illustrate.

The first notification of an actual or suspected homicide comes into the police department. The caller states that she heard screams and shots fired. The officer receiving the call should log the exact time the call came in; make a note of the exact location of the occurrence; ask whether the perpetrator, a suspicious person, or a vehicle is still at the scene; find out where the caller is, whether she'll remain at the scene, and, if not, where she can be contacted; and log the name, address, and phone number of the caller. The officer may, when practical (and if the person seems calm and of suitable age), request the caller's assistance in safeguarding the location of the occurrence—for example, by seeing that no one other than law enforcement personnel is admitted and especially that nothing is touched. The officer should, as soon as possible, write down word for word what the caller said. (Many communities have equipment to automatically record calls to police.) Officers are aware—and statistics bear this out—that the individual who reported the incident may later become a suspect.

Based on station-house protocol and an assessment of the caller's information, the dispatcher will send enough personnel and equipment to handle the situation. With a suspected homicide, the dispatcher will notify his or her supervisor and, in turn, the homicide/detective unit.

The first officer on the scene is a uniformed patrol officer who has responded to a radio transmission or emergency call. The scene of a homicide can be fairly orderly, extremely chaotic, or somewhere in between.

A responding officer could be met by a calm, composed individual who directs him or her to the body, which displays obvious signs of death and lies in an easily secured location. At the other end of the spectrum, the officer might find a crowd of hysterical people milling about, the scene may be a public place, and the perpetrator may still be present; or the victim may still be alive and in need of medical assistance. For purposes of illustration, we'll use a scenario closer to the first. But professionals know that when responding to a report of a violent crime, they should expect the unexpected.

The police officer's first regard is life; he or she determines whether the victim is alive or dead. (Only one officer should enter the immediate crime area to view the victim, and using only one path of entry and exit.) If the perpetrator is still present, the officer tries to apprehend him or her. Otherwise, the officer radios that the perpetrator has escaped and detains any witnesses or suspects. If an ambulance was already present when he or she arrived, the officer must find out whether anyone has moved the body or any items within the crime scene. If items were moved, the officer records what they are, why they were moved, and who did the moving. He or she should also document the names, serial numbers, and hospital affiliation of the ambulance crew present.

Protection of the crime scene is crucial. A good officer heeds a long list of don'ts: he or she will not touch, move, or alter anything; use the telephone, flush toilets, or run tap water in sinks or bathtubs; smoke at the crime scene; and, above all, allow others in or out. (In real life, however, any number of factors can complicate the job of preserving the physical evidence—inclement weather when the crime scene is outdoors, the presence of the media or a crowd of onlookers, an armed or hostage-holding perpetrator, or hysterical witnesses, to mention but a few.)

As other uniformed officers arrive, they establish

and secure a perimeter with physical barriers such as tape, ropes, or cones. They record the names, addresses, dates of birth, and telephone numbers of all persons at the crime scene. They move all persons from the immediate area—being careful not to chase off witnesses or the perpetrator, who may still be present.

Soon, the homicide detectives arrive. They assess the crime scene, noting a host of details. Have any alterations to the crime scene been made as a matter of investigative necessity? Are lights turned on or off? Are doors open, closed, locked, or unlocked? Where was the body found? Where was it in relation to windows and furniture? What is the victim wearing? Are gas, appliances, or a motor vehicle turned on or off?

Crime is a confusing, costly, and harrowing matter. And the investigation has only begun.

Forensic investigators remove the body of a homicide victim from a house. An array of specialists will examine and run tests on the body to find out the circumstances of death.

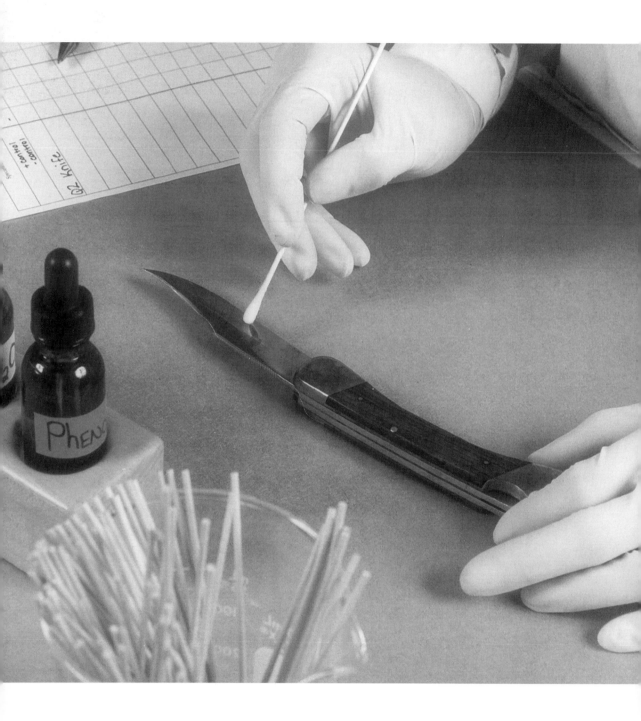

BODY
MATERIALS
AND FLUIDS

*W*esley began a new page of notes. When he paused, he looked at me. "Dr. Scarpetta, if she was killed shortly after she was abducted, how decomposed should she have been when she was found on October seventh?"

"Under the conditions described, I would expect her to be moderately decomposed," I said. "I would also expect insect activity, possibly other postmortem damage, depending on how accessible her body was to carnivores."

"In other words, she should be in a lot worse shape than this"—he tapped photographs—"if she'd been dead six days."

"More decomposed than this, yes."

This scene, from Patricia Cornwell's book *The Body Farm*, illustrates the importance of correctly estimating the time of death in a homicide investigation. Time of death is a crucial factor in a murder case. Establishing it can eliminate a suspect, break an alibi, or help convict

If this presumptive test establishes that the stain on the knife is actually blood, further tests will be run to determine blood type and serum enzymes and proteins.

a murderer. In general, three sources can be used to determine the time of death: witnesses; associated events, including what are commonly referred to as "scene markers," such as newspapers, letters, or TV schedules; and *postmortem*, or after-death, changes in the body.

To understand the changes that occur after death, it helps to know how the body sustains life. When we breathe, we take oxygen into our lungs, which the circulatory system in turn supplies to all the body's tissues via blood cells. The body also has systems for eliminating waste products and defending itself from the bacteria and germs that are always present. At death, all these systems stop. Consequently, bacteria begin to thrive and grow, releasing enzymes that dissolve the body from the inside and produce gas. In addition, the blood turns a dark purplish color from the loss of oxygen, and under the pull of gravity it settles to the lowest or underside portions of the body. Muscles begin to stiffen.

Medical experts can estimate time of death, and sometimes glean other clues, from the phenomena of *postmortem lividity* and *rigor mortis*. Postmortem lividity, also called *livor mortis*, is a purplish "liver" discoloration on the part of the body facing the ground. (The part of the body facing up appears pale.) Caused by the pooling of blood within blood vessels from the effect of gravity, lividity begins about 30 minutes after death. If, in the early stages of lividity, an investigator presses a finger firmly against the discolored skin, the pressure will cause "blanching." When pressure is released, the discoloration returns. Four or five hours after death, however, the discoloration becomes clotted and pressure will no longer cause blanching. A related phenomenon, *fixed lividity*, can also provide important clues. Lividity becomes "fixed" in 8 to 10 hours, meaning that if the body has remained in the same position for that period of time, the *livor mortis* can no longer be significantly shifted by changing the position of the body. Consequently, if lividity is observed on the back of a body found lying face down, investigators can be sure that the body was turned over after death and was possibly even moved from another site.

Immediately following death, the muscles relax and then become rigid without the shortening of the muscle. Rigor mortis, the stiffening of a body, manifests itself within the first two to four hours. Stiffening is first noticeable in very small muscles, including the eyelids, face, and lower jaw. It then spreads to the neck and the rest of the body.

After rigor mortis has spread throughout the entire body, involving all the muscles, it begins to disappear in the same order that it first became noticeable—small muscles first, followed by large muscles. After about 48 to 60 hours, all the muscles are again relaxed. This is due to decomposition of the muscle fibers.

While short-term postmortem changes follow a fairly predictable course, they are affected by such factors as where the body is found—in water, buried in soil, or in the desert, for example. In addition, numerous environmental factors can affect the rate at which decomposition occurs over longer periods—and complicate efforts to determine when a person died. Temperature and humidity are two key variables. Low temperatures and low humidity slow decomposition; high temperatures and humidity accelerate it. The bodies of early polar explorers who died a century and a half ago have been found under layers of ice, preserved as if they had died yesterday. On the other hand, in a moist, tropical climate, a corpse left outside can become skeletonized in a few weeks. In part this is because such a climate is ideal for insects that feed on decomposing flesh.

Knowledge of insects' habits has helped solve many crimes. One story, from the book *Bones*, by Dr. Douglas Ubelaker and Henry Scammell, is an apt illustration of the significance of insects and death. The body of a woman was discovered on a trail in a wooded area near the District of Columbia. There appeared to be no evidence of foul play, but, following routine police procedure, photographs were taken of the scene. It was late summer, and the dead woman was dressed in a tube top and slacks. Her clothes were intact, which reduced the possibility that she had been sexually assaulted.

Despite the peaceful surroundings, the advanced stage of decomposition meant that the medical examiner would have to steel himself for a grisly task. Maggots—the larvae of flies—were in the eyes, around the nose and mouth, in the chest area, and on the palms of both hands. The woman, the medical examiner believed, had been dead for about 10 to 12 days. She was identified immediately, and because of the condition of the body, pressure was put on the authorities to release her corpse for a speedy burial. After a limited autopsy, the cause of death was listed as unknown, and

Insect Detectives

Forensic entomology, the study of insects associated with death, can be a valuable tool in homicide investigations. Because the scent of a corpse attracts insects and triggers predictable insect activity, and because the life cycles of the various insects on the body are fixed and precise, forensic entomologists can work backward to accurately estimate time of death. Bug behavior can also indicate whether the victim was killed indoors or out, during the day or night, in warm or cold weather, in shade or sun.

The following is a time line of insect activity:

10 minutes	Ten minutes after the body is dead in open air, flies arrive and lay thousands of eggs in the mouth, nose, and eyes of the corpse.
12 hours	Eggs hatch and maggots feed on tissues.
24–36 hours	Beetles arrive and feast on the dry skin.
48 hours	Spiders, mites, and millipedes arrive to feed on the bugs that are there.

Excerpted from *Cause of Death* © 1992 by Keith D. Wilson.
Used with permission of Writer's Digest Books, a division of F & W Publications, Inc.

Maggots, the larvae of flies, swarm over a deer carcass. Insect activity on a corpse provides a reliable method for establishing when a person died.

the body was turned over to the undertaker.

Typically, that would have ended the investigation, but one detective couldn't get the case out of his mind. What bothered him most was a discrepancy about the time of death: the victim had been reported missing just a few days before her body was discovered on the trail, yet the medical examiner had estimated that she'd been dead for 10 to 12 days. Finally, three years later, the detective got in touch with a forensic anthropologist, showed him the photographs, and asked for a second opinion.

Anthropologist Bill Rodriguez asked all the normal questions and studied the photographs. He told the detective that considering the time of year, the larval activity in the photographs was consistent with the medical examiner's time-of-death estimate. As he handed back the photos, Rodriguez asked if police had a suspect. The detective said they didn't. He explained that the lack of evidence of violence had led them to rule out murder.

"Of course there's evidence," Rodriguez said, pointing to the pictures. "You just showed it to me." Because of his forensic training, he had immediately recognized the significance of the larval activity in the palms of the hands. Although the remaining surfaces on both arms were clearly free of maggots, the flies had laid their eggs in the deep lesions across the width of the woman's palms. This signifies the kind of injury that is typically sustained by someone defending against a knife attack.

The detective was stunned. "But how can you be sure the hand injuries aren't just something that happened when she fell?"

Rodriguez shook his head. He pointed to the chest area in the top photo. The decomposition, he said, suggested something else. "Maggots don't swarm like that unless they have something to feed on. . . . Look at the body, I think you're going to find she was stabbed in the chest."

After much persuasion, the detective convinced his superiors to reopen the case. The body was exhumed by lantern light in the middle of a snowstorm. This time the examination was more thorough. Soft tissue was simmered away gently for a clearer view. Unmistakable blade patterns were found on the bones of the hands and in the chest. A new death certificate was issued, with the manner of death reclassified to homicide. Because there is no statute of limitations on murder, the case will remain open until the killer is found.

🐜   🐜   🐜

There is a key principle in homicide investigation called "theoretical exchange." It states that during a murderous encounter, traces of the people and the place are likely to be transferred to one another. Specifically, the perpetrator will take away traces of the victim and

Scraping a towel for evidence that may have been trapped by body fluids.

the crime scene; the victim will retain traces of the perpetrator and the crime scene (which becomes important if the body is moved to a different location); and the perpetrator will leave traces of himself or herself at the crime scene. Hence, the cardinal rule for investigators is to protect and preserve the crime scene, which can yield crucial evidence.

Body fluids are often among the most important evidence available from theoretical exchange. Water or fluid makes up about 92 percent of our bodies. And the analysis of certain types of body fluids—blood, spittle or

1

A forensic scientist visually examines a pair of jeans for any holes, tears, or stains.

saliva, sweat, semen, and urine—can provide information about the person from which they came.

Each of us has one of four blood types—A, B, AB, or O—which we inherited from our parents. Blood type can be determined from a sample. Obviously, however, because there are only four blood types, hundreds of millions of people share the same one. Matching blood type alone would not help to prove a suspect's guilt. But blood also contains enzymes and proteins, which are collectively known as genetic markers and which differ from person to person, and labs can identify these chemicals in a blood sample. For example, the enzyme phosphoglucomutase, or PGM, is found in everyone's blood, but at least 10 different types of PGM have been identified. Two people may share the same blood type,

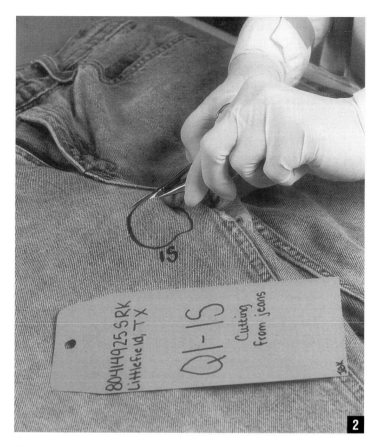

2

A piece of fabric containing a stain presumptively identified as semen is cut out. It will be sent to another lab for further tests.

but statistically it is much less likely they will share a blood type and a PGM marker. To date, scientists have identified 12 different genetic markers in blood, each of them containing between 3 and 10 chemical types. Rarely are all 12 genetic markers identified in one blood sample, but even finding just 3 or 4 identical markers in two samples raises the odds that the samples came from different people to a million to one—in some cases, 100 million to one. In other words, there is only a very small chance that two people will have the same blood type with the same chemical combination.

Well-prepared homicide units maintain a portable homicide kit to assist them in the collection and documentation of crime-scene evidence. Body material collections are best performed by crime-scene technicians and other experts who have been trained in forensic science techniques. At a crime scene, such experts can collect pools or small amounts of wet blood in eyedroppers or hypodermic syringes and then transfer the blood to sterile containers. When dried blood is present on a nonporous surface (even in small amounts), technicians can scrape it off using a clean razor blade or a sterile scalpel. Small items containing dried blood are bagged and sent to the lab. Traces or smears can be picked up with a 100% cotton swab or gauze pad moistened with distilled water. Other body fluids can be collected the same way, with the paramount concern always that each sample be put in a separate, sterile container.

In some cases, the hands of the deceased are bagged to preserve any trace evidence that may be found under the fingernails, which will be examined during autopsy. Paper rather than plastic bags are used because plastic tends to accelerate putrification, a process whereby the gases and other properties from postmortem decomposition distort and swell body tissues.

Any physiological fluid found at the scene, such as urine, feces, perspiration, ear wax, and nasal mucus, can be typed for a blood grouping, providing the material comes from a *secretor*. A secretor is a person whose blood type can be determined from body fluids other than blood. Experts believe that between 60 and 80 percent of the population are secretors. For reasons that are unknown but probably have a genetic basis, a nonsecretor's blood type can be determined only from a blood sample.

But body materials other than fluids can provide clues to a suspect's identity, regardless of secretor status. Hair is considered a *class characteristic*. A single hair cannot positively identify a given suspect, but it can be classified as similar to a known sample. In addition, analysis of hair found at a crime scene can determine species type (animal or human); race; location of growth (head, chest, pubis, and so on); whether the hair was dyed or treated in any way; and how it was removed (for example, pulled or cut). Tests can also reveal whether the subject suffers from certain diseases or has abused drugs. Plus, sex and genetic markers can be determined from a hair root, and blood can be typed from the shaft. Body tissues are picked up with tweezers, packaged, and sent along to the medical examiner.

♠   ♠   ♠

Writer David Fisher, who shadowed Federal Bureau of Investigation (FBI) scientists for his book *Hard Evidence*, recounts a case where blood evidence told its own tale. A young married woman from a small Tennessee town, Maynardville, was abducted and beaten to death. The prime suspect was a friend of the victim's husband, but there was little physical evidence to link him to the murder. The fact that he was in their house often meant any fingerprints and hairs found on the premises weren't significant. But when police searched his own house, they found the new jeans he'd been wearing the day of the murder.

Examination of jeans often proves difficult. The blue dyes used in the manufacturing process will usually render any testing useless. This time, however, investigators got lucky. As they turned the pants inside out to cut them open at the seams, a dime-sized bloodstain was found in one of the cotton pockets. The suspect claimed he'd been in a fistfight and had skinned his knuckles.

All 12 enzyme system tests were run on the sample, but scientists could get results only on five or six of them. It was determined that three of the enzymes could not possibly have come from the suspect; they were, however, consistent with the makeup of the victim's blood. Investigators assumed he'd punched the victim and then unknowingly put his hand into the cotton pocket. That's what the court heard when the evidence was presented at trial, and ultimately the suspect was convicted.

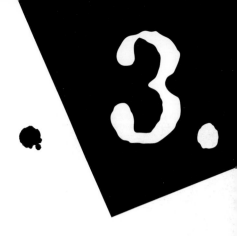

THE AUTOPSY

Dr. Harriet Burns slipped into her surgical scrubs, pulled plastic booties over her shoes, and turned to her assistant, Mark Harper. Harper held out a sterile latex glove, into which Burns thrust her right hand. The process was repeated for her left hand.

Burns, a medical examiner, was readying for an autopsy. In the cold, green-tiled enclosure, with its shiny stainless-steel sink and tables, the voices of the two colleagues resonated, having a chilling effect on conversation. The detective on the case, Parkins, was a silent observer. Near the table where the corpse lay, Harper tested and adjusted the microphone, then turned his attention to the tray alongside the table. A pathologist's panoply of tools were arranged in neat rows, along with several types of physician's saws. In addition, there were vials, jars, and a toe tag all numbered and labeled with the name of the deceased.

Forensic anthropologist Dr. William Bass with a skull and other bones. From skeletal remains, forensic anthropologists can determine sex, estimate age, and frequently specify cause of death.

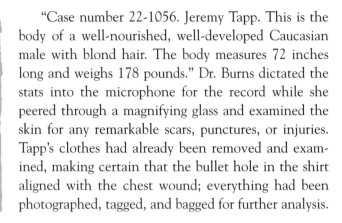

"Case number 22-1056. Jeremy Tapp. This is the body of a well-nourished, well-developed Caucasian male with blond hair. The body measures 72 inches long and weighs 178 pounds." Dr. Burns dictated the stats into the microphone for the record while she peered through a magnifying glass and examined the skin for any remarkable scars, punctures, or injuries. Tapp's clothes had already been removed and examined, making certain that the bullet hole in the shirt aligned with the chest wound; everything had been photographed, tagged, and bagged for further analysis.

The medical examiner's or coroner's office is charged with investigating violent, sudden, unexpected, or suspicious deaths. In addition to all homicides, such cases include deaths by suicide, accident, poisoning, and criminal violence; the deaths of all persons in legal detention or jails; and sudden death of individuals in apparently good health. Investigations are also conducted when the cause of death may be a disease that could pose a threat to public health, when the deceased was undergoing medical treatment or a surgical procedure, and when a body is unclaimed.

The basic tool of any death investigation is the autopsy, an examination of the body. There are two kinds of death investigation and two types of autopsy. A *medical autopsy* is generally performed in a hospital by a pathologist as a scientific examination to determine the cause of death. A *medicolegal autopsy* is ordered by legal authorities, usually the medical examiner, to ensure justice and to determine the cause of death under the circumstances listed above. Ordinarily, a police representative, the investigating detective on the case, will be present as a witness from the crime scene. The detective can contribute any information that might be pertinent to the investigation. For example, certain changes that take place during transportation and storage may be subject to misinterpretation.

In one case the deceased's face was flattened, giving the impression that the body had been found face down. In reality, the killer had placed a heavy piece of furniture on the victim's face after death. This kind of anomaly is what is called a *postmortem artifact,* and the detective's presence at the autopsy helped avoid any confusion or misinterpretation on the part of the pathologist. Besides, requiring a police officer to attend the autopsy ensures the identification of the body for the *chain of custody:* detailing the evidence as it passes from hand to hand. At every stage of the investigation, the body has been measured, labeled, photographed, and perhaps

Medical Examiner, Coroner, or Pathologist —What's the Difference?

Who determines if the bruises on a body's neck are due to strangulation? Who can tell us if a wound marks a bullet's entrance or its exit? Who can say whether a badly burned body was dead or alive at the time of the fire, or whether a newborn found in a garbage can ever breathed on its own or arrived stillborn?

Not just any doctor could answer these questions, for few medical school graduates today get any exposure to forensic medicine. And while the titles medical examiner, coroner, and pathologist may mean the same thing to the layperson, there are some key distinctions.

A **coroner** is the oldest-known court officer. The title is a holdover from the British criminal law system; the position of coroner was institutionalized during the time of Richard the Lion-Hearted. There were no professional qualifications for the post of coroner, and the position in early America was often that of a funeral director. Nowadays, coroners are usually elected, although in some states they are appointed. Also, in some jurisdictions the coroner is not even a physician but is still officially responsible for taking legal charge of the body.

A **pathologist** is a doctor qualified in the study of the anatomy of disease. Through the dissection of bodies after death, the pathologist hopes to discover the cause of disease and the nature of its manifestations. A pathologist may or may not be a medical examiner.

A **medical examiner** typically is a forensic pathologist and acts as a forensic expert who plays a vitally important part of the investigative team. The procedures used in the official medicolegal investigation of death fall under the supervision of the chief medical examiner or the coroner of the district. A medical examiner determines the *cause* (the pathological condition), the *manner* (the physical agent), and the *mode* (intentional or accidental) of death, and searches for clues as to who the killer is.

X-rayed to aid the determinations.

The series of steps for the medicolegal autopsy include

- examination of the crime scene
- identification of the body and tagging
- external examination of the body, including an accurate, detailed description of all wounds
- dissection and internal examination
- toxicological examination of body fluids and organs for evidence of drugs, alcohol, poisons, and so on.

Since the medical examiner's case begins at the examination of the crime scene, we'll talk a little more about what happens there. Identification provides a starting point and acts as a source of direction for an investigation. In many cases relatives or acquaintances will be present who can make an identification of the body at the scene. Wise investigators, however, will pursue established practices of identification. The body is photographed, often a complete sketch is made, a description of both the body and clothing is prepared, and a request for medical and dental records is issued in addition to a request for blood-typing and fingerprints of the deceased. Identifying corpses is not always an easy task. If the body is mutilated, has been left in the wild, or is decomposed, there are additional problems.

The most logical sources for identification can be the clothes and possessions of the deceased. A driver's license, social security card, or any photo I.D. card can serve as a good tentative means of verifying identity. Pockets are thoroughly searched and their contents ordered and photographed. In addition, certain laundry marks or dry-cleaning tags by commercial cleaners can be traced to specific locations and thus to customers.

Distinctive pieces of jewelry can be identified as belonging to a certain individual; watches, bands, and bracelets may carry inscriptions. More expensive watches will have a mark identifying the particular craftsman. Also, publicizing any exceptional material possessions in local papers or on television often leads to additional clues.

Fingerprints are one of the best methods of identification. Even if the deceased does not have fingerprints on file, a comparison and match of the deceased's prints with fingerprints lifted from his or her home or place of business can prove sufficient individuality.

Obtaining the prints from a body can sometimes be another matter. In many cases, the fingerprint card is cut into strips. The fingers are inked, or a black fingerprint powder is used, and then each finger is pressed onto the strip in its corresponding box. When rigidity is present in the fingers, the examiner may have to bend the joints back and forth until they are sufficiently flexible.

If the body is shriveled or mummified, the fingers are amputated and immersed in softening solution or water until the skin softens. Each finger is placed in a separate, numbered bottle, with great care being exercised not to mix them up. When circumstances require these extreme measures, the medical examiner almost always does the work personally.

At the other extreme, if the body is a "floater"—if it has been immersed in water for a long time—another procedure may have to be employed. If the fingers are shriveled or wrinkled but still intact, fluid can be injected into the finger with a fine needle or hypodermic syringe in order to restore the finger's

A prominent investigator tells the story of a man who was shot and killed by his potential victims during a narcotics robbery. The police arrested the would-be victims, along with a female accomplice of the dead man, and seized a gun and other evidence. The woman gave police a fictitious name for the deceased. Later, when fingerprints were taken during autopsy, the results were mistakenly put in the dead file under the fictitious name. No records check was made. At the same time, a separate investigation was undertaken because the gun used in the aborted stickup was the same caliber used in three New York City homicides during similar robberies. The city police detectives took an additional set of prints to compare to those obtained during the homicide investigation, and a records check ensued. The gun was also tested for ballistics and positively identified as the weapon used in the three homicides. Finally, the results of a new records check revealed that the dead man was not the person named by the accomplice. He was, in fact, a wanted escapee who, along with his female partner, had already been identified as a murder suspect. Her intentions, obviously, were to direct police away from her role in the murders. If not for the second fingerprint records check, she would have succeeded. The lesson: the original prints should never have been filed before a follow-up records check.

Getting fingerprints from a victim who has been submerged in water for a long time:

1 *Fluid is injected to restore the normal contours of the shriveled fingertip.*

2 *The finger is cut off so that it can be rolled.*

3 *The inked finger is rolled on a fingerprint card.*

normal contour, and the print can then be taken. This is called rehydration. Sometimes the skin will be so loose it will come off the hand like a glove. In that case, each tip is placed in a separate water-filled test tube, which is sealed and sent to a crime laboratory, often at the FBI. In the past a technician might, under certain conditions, remove the skin and place it over his or her own gloved finger, then roll the skin for prints.

Teeth provide another excellent form of identification. The scientific application of dentistry to legal matters is called *forensic odontology*. Forensic odontologists are consulted in matters of identification especially when antemortem (before-death) dental records are available or when bite marks might be matched to a particular person; they are also called in when the victim has dental and oral injuries. Through X rays, the use of powerful cameras, and available medical records, the forensic odontologist can provide informa-

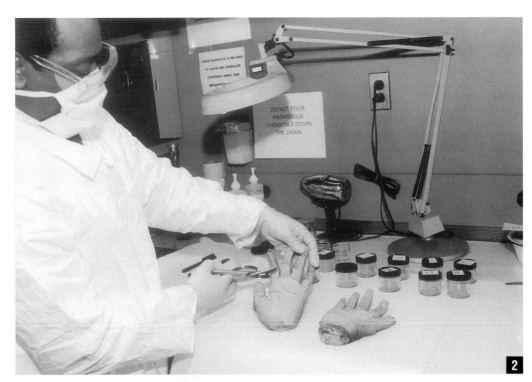

tion about the deceased that the investigator can use for positive identification, including age, race, certain facial characteristics, socioeconomic group status, occupation, and habits.

No discussion of autopsy procedures would be complete without considerable attention to the work of *forensic toxicologists*. Toxicologists are responsible for detecting the presence of, and then identifying, drugs and poisons in body fluids, tissues, and organs.

In a special for the cable TV network HBO, Dr. Michael Baden, a famous criminalist, described an interesting case highlighting the role of toxicology. Baden was called in by the Occupational Safety and Health Administration (OSHA) to help investigate the death of a 33-year-old man named Robert Curley. Several months after starting a new job at a university, Curley, who had been married for only a year, entered a hospital half-delirious. His body, he said, felt as though it were on fire, and the pain was so bad he had to be restrained. Curley later died in the hospital of unknown causes.

His youth, combined with the tragedy of his new wife's loss and the mystery of his death, left the community shocked and clamoring for answers. For some time, however, authorities couldn't say why Curley had died.

Toxicological tests eventually identified the cause of death as thallium poisoning. Thallium, an extremely rare element, is used primarily as a pesticide and in making photoelectric cells. It belongs to a class of poisonous elements known as heavy metals, which the forensic toxicologist only occasionally encounters. Dr. Richard Saferstein, a forensic science consultant in Mount Laurel, New Jersey, describes how the presence of heavy metals is detected. "To screen for many of these metals," he says, "the investigator may dissolve the suspect body fluid or tissue in a hydrochloric acid solution and insert a copper strip into the solution." This is called the Reinsch test. "The appearance of a sil-

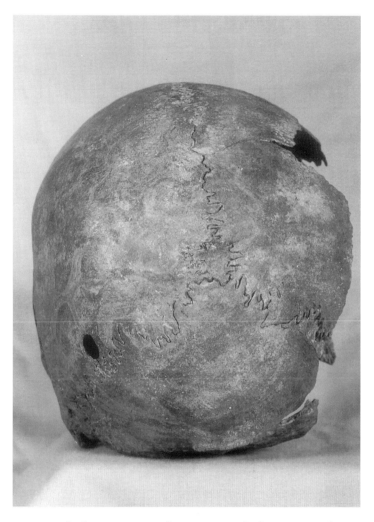

The irregular lines between the curved bones of the skull, called sutures, begin to fill and fuse as a person gets older. Because this process follows a predictable pattern, sutures enable forensic anthropologists to estimate age at death. This skull also tells the story of a violent death: the hole in the lower left portion is where a bullet entered; the shattered portion at right, where it exited.

very or dark coating in the copper," Saferstein explains, "is indicative of the presence of a heavy metal."

When they heard about the toxicology results, Curley's former coworkers at the university became alarmed. Perhaps they, too, were being exposed to thallium. OSHA investigators took air samples and swabbed different areas around the workplace for traces of the element. They found five bottles containing thallium, yet no other university workers appeared to have been affected. The fatal levels in Robert Curley's body still could not be explained.

Attention shifted to possible sources other than the university—and to the possibility of intentional poisoning. Might Curley have received a fatal dose of thallium in the hospital where he died? Who could have administered it? Investigators also decided to test close friends and relatives of the victim to see whether they, too, had elevated levels of thallium. They found that his wife, Joanne, had above-normal levels, as did her four-year-old daughter. Investigators also found traces of thallium in Curley's thermos. They developed a list of 26 possible suspects.

Three years after his death, on August 23, 1994, authorities exhumed Robert Curley's body to check his hair for the presence of thallium. Curley's hair was dissolved in acid and vaporized. This enabled investigators to read a "time line" held within the shaft of the hair. They determined that the poison was present six months before Curley began working at the university. And he had received the largest dose just a few days before he died in the hospital. Investigators eliminated all but one of the 26 suspects: Joanne Curley. She finally confessed. She had killed her husband, she said, for his money—Curley's net worth had been approximately $300,000—and had begun poisoning him just two months after they were married. An important point to the story is this: had Robert Curley been cremated with no autopsy findings, her crime would have gone unpunished.

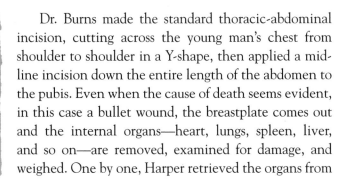

Dr. Burns made the standard thoracic-abdominal incision, cutting across the young man's chest from shoulder to shoulder in a Y-shape, then applied a midline incision down the entire length of the abdomen to the pubis. Even when the cause of death seems evident, in this case a bullet wound, the breastplate comes out and the internal organs—heart, lungs, spleen, liver, and so on—are removed, examined for damage, and weighed. One by one, Harper retrieved the organs from the swinging scale and sliced tissue samples from each for chemical and toxicological analysis. The bullet was finally recovered from inside the chest cavity and saved for another lab. Tapp's stomach was then removed, its contents reserved for other lab tests. The presence of food can help investigators determine what—and when—the deceased last ate.

Throughout the autopsy, Harper siphoned off fluids from all the body cavities as well as the urine present in the bladder, which, upon analysis, would indicate whether Jeremy Tapp was on drugs. The genitalia were examined for evidence of injury or foreign matter. With suspected sex homicides, vaginal and anal swabs are also collected so that tests can be run for the presence of seminal fluid.

Finally, Tapp's head and brain were examined. While Dr. Burns checked the victim's scalp for injuries, Harper took scrapings from under his fingernails, clipped the nails, and deposited the clippings into a vial for the trace-evidence tests. If the deceased fought with his assailant, there could be tissue, blood, or particles of fiber evidence under the nails.

Eyes and eyelids were examined next. Dr. Burns was looking for *petechiae*, pinpoint hemorrhages that appear in cases of asphyxia, strangulation, or hanging. An incision was made across the top of the head, through the scalp, and extending from ear to ear. A flap of scalp was pulled down in front of the face to allow the skull to be sawed open and the brain removed for examination. This can be a disturbing sight for the detective, but when Dr. Burns replaced the skull section and pulled the hair and scalp back into place, the face and head were ready to be prepared for the funeral with no damage visible.

Dr. Burns placed the internal organs back into the body cavity, and Harper began sewing the body up. The physical autopsy had taken a little less than two hours. The investigation would now shift to the out-

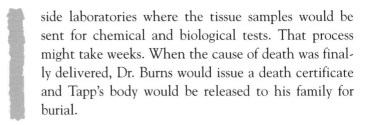

side laboratories where the tissue samples would be sent for chemical and biological tests. That process might take weeks. When the cause of death was finally delivered, Dr. Burns would issue a death certificate and Tapp's body would be released to his family for burial.

Identifying the deceased is generally the best starting point for a death investigation. But what happens when investigators have just a skeleton? Or when a body has been burned or damaged beyond recognition? How can they possibly determine the deceased's identity? Under circumstances such as these, a *forensic anthropologist* will be called in.

Forensic anthropologists study the remains of the dead not only for clues to the cause of the subject's death but also for details about the subject's life. This can give investigators a place to start their inquiry. From skeletal remains alone an anthropologist can tell whether the person was male or female. This is judged primarily by examining the pelvis, the jawbone, the skull, and the forehead. For example, a female pelvis is wider and lower. (The pubis and sacrum, the lower part of the vertebral column, will also tell whether she delivered a child in her lifetime.) A male's skull is thicker and heavier and has a more prominent brow ridge.

A forensic anthropologist can also estimate the subject's age at death from the extent of *ossification,* or bone formation. *Epiphyses,* the expanded, jointed ends of long bones, develop separately from the shafts of the bones but later in life fuse with them. Another determining factor for estimating age is the skull, which is composed of several curved bones joined together by irregular lines called *sutures.* As we approach our twenties, these sutures begin to fill up with bone and close. This process continues as we grow older and follows a distinct pattern.

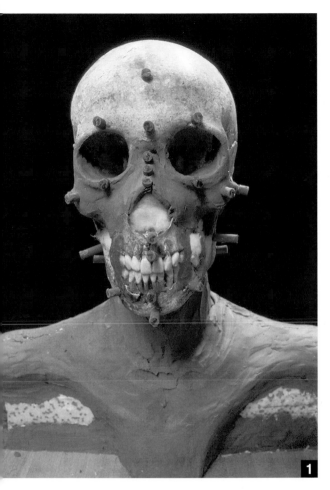
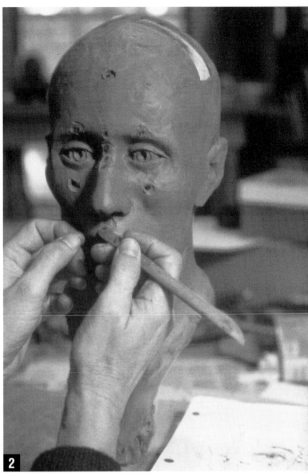

Other information a forensic anthropologist might get from a skeleton includes:

- **Height.** This estimate is based on the length of the long leg bones and arm bones.
- **Weight and handedness.** By examining the muscle attachments to the bones, and the stress and wear on bones at certain points, weight can be surmised. Also, by comparing the arm bones, the forensic anthropologist can determine whether the person was right- or left-handed. The bones of the dominant arm are slightly longer, and the scapula (shoul-

Forensic facial reconstruction.

1 *Skull with pegs that indicate the depth of soft tissue.*
2 *Clay is applied and carefully modeled to create facial features.*

der blade) and clavicle (collarbone) also help indicate handedness.

- **Racial group.** This is determined by examining the width and height of the nose and using statistical procedures to measure skull dimensions. Because of mixed racial heritage there are a lot of variables, and computers are often used to sort out all the numbers.
- **Occupation.** A flute-player's teeth, palate, and bones around the mouth will have been affected by her work. A carpenter's teeth may be chipped from putting nails in his mouth. The spine of a manual laborer may show signs of having carried heavy loads.
- **Signs of violent death.** Signs of trauma—cut marks, blows to the skull, broken bones—and bullets or pellets in or near the body are good indicators of violence. If the person was strangled, the bone in the throat will be fractured. In addition, if a person died as a result of a metallic poison, the poison can still be extracted from the bones years later.

●   ●   ●

On a hot day in August 1995, in the Sycamore Canyon Wilderness area of Yavapai County, Arizona, a hiker found more than he'd expected. Along a knife-edged ridge several hundred yards up the mountain from the main trailhead, the hiker stumbled across human skeletal remains. The portion of the canyon where the remains were lying is extremely rugged, a difficult climb for even the fittest and most experienced. Perhaps only a dozen hikers a year venture off the main trailhead in this area. For a woman nine months pregnant, the climb would be virtually impossible.

Dr. Laura Fulginiti, a forensic anthropologist in Maricopa County, determined that the skeleton was that of a white female between 25 and 40 years old, 5' 2" to 5' 5" tall. Dr. Fulginiti also verified that the victim was at or near full-term pregnancy at the time of her death; a full fetal skeleton was recovered with the adult. Someone must have been missing this woman.

We know that forensic anthropologists try to analyze the story the bones tell. In a similar way, forensic reconstruction artists provide a facial facsimile that brings life and likeness to a skull.

The forensic sculptor glues pencil-eraser-sized rubber cylinders at 26 key points on the surface of a skull. Each peg indicates the depth of muscle and facial tissue that would be present for specific racial groups, estimating the "soft tissue" of the face. With the pegs as a guideline, plasticine is laid in lattice-work patterns and modeling clay is then applied, filling in all the recessed areas. Glass or plastic eyes are affixed in the sockets and the details of the face—nose, brow, lips, and ears—are carefully designed. A combination of technical, artistic, and anatomical know-how, with an added measure of imagination, are needed to re-create a face. The reconstruction is then photographed and distributed to the press.

Reproductions are not intended for the eyes of strangers. They are meant to trigger a response from someone who knew the person, perhaps a friend or relative. A 75 percent success rate attests to the fact that facial reconstruction, sometimes referred to as "faces from the grave," is a powerful tool for helping identify the unknowns.

Investigators in Yavapai County know that while three out of four is pretty good odds, it's no guarantee. But they're hoping that someone, somewhere, will recognize the facial reconstruction of the pregnant woman found in the Sycamore Canyon Wilderness area. Someone must be missing this woman. Someone could come forward and help investigators give a name to the face. Someone could help them put the mystery to rest.

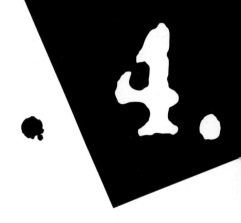

Objects
as Clues

If you were to dump a handful of pennies on a table and examine them closely, you might notice something surprising. No two are identical. Some will have different dates, of course, and it is likely that not all will bear the same mint letter. But even among coins minted in the same year at the same location, you'll notice small variations in thickness, color, shine, and wear.

Our world is a place of breathtaking variety, where you'd be hard-pressed to find *any* two objects that are exactly the same. In a very real way, it is only our ability to *exclude* minor variations and to perceive the essential similarity of objects in a particular class that enables us to think, to communicate with one another, and to deal with and make sense of our everyday experiences.

When we buy a 98¢ candy bar with a dollar, it really doesn't matter which two pennies we get as change, but for a criminal investigator, the small, subtle, and

Photographing a handgun where it was dropped after a shooting. In addition to any fingerprints found on the gun, ballistics tests will provide investigators and prosecutors with key evidence.

sometimes invisible variations among objects can make all the difference. In many cases the name of the game in crime-solving, unlike everyday life, is not to group like objects together, but to individualize them.

To a *forensic ballistics* expert, each firearm and each bullet is a unique object, and each crime scene where a gun was used holds a variety of clues from which a picture of a specific set of events can be constructed. The word *ballistics*—from the Latin *ballista*, a type of giant crossbow or catapult used in ancient times—originally referred to the study of missiles in flight and of projectile motion. Over time, however, the term has come to refer exclusively to firearms. For our purposes here, ballistics is the study of firearms and bullets used in the detection and identification of weapons used in crimes.

Although ballistics represents one of the oldest applications of science to crime-solving—the first case of a bullet being used to connect an individual to a crime dates back to 1835 in London—two significant advances helped establish its lasting importance as a forensic science. The first advance occurred with the 1927 invention, by Phillip Gravelle, of the *comparison microscope*. Basically, the comparison microscope consists of two compound microscopes combined into one binocular unit through a bridge that incorporates a series of mirrors. The viewer sees a circular field divided down the middle by a thin line, and two objects can be compared side by side. The second advance involved a pair of developments: a microscope that measured a fired bullet's ridges and grooves, and the *helixometer,* a lighted telescope that could be inserted into the barrel of a weapon, which was developed by the physicist John Fisher in the 1920s.

In order to appreciate these developments, it's important to understand how a gun works. A gun has a hole, or bore, drilled in the barrel, which the bullet travels through; a gun barrel is essentially a metal tube. With the exception of shotguns, all weapons are rifled—that is, they have a series of wide spiral grooves cut into the inside of the barrel. The raised area between the grooves is called the land. The purpose of rifling is to spin the cigar-shaped bullet in flight—much as a properly thrown football spins—keeping it gyroscopically correct and thus accurate. The arrangement of lands and grooves and the twist of spiraling varies among the different makes and models of guns.

A live round of ammunition, called a cartridge, has the following components: projectile, primer, gunpowder, and cartridge case. The cartridge case contains the ignition system, a powder charge, and the projectile or bullet. When a gun is fired, the firing pin hits the primer, causing the gunpowder inside to explode, which in turn causes the bullet to rapidly separate from the case. The spent cartridge remains in the chamber of a revolver (semiautomatic guns eject the case after firing).

As the bullet travels down the gun's barrel at high speed, the spiral markings from the barrel get etched into it. These rifling characteristics are called *striations*. No two rifled barrels, even those manufactured in suc-

Television blunders

Did you ever see a television detective collect a firearm by sticking a pen or pencil down the barrel? For real detectives, that is definitely a no-no. First of all, it's not safe. Second, the most important information that can be obtained from a gun is often inside the barrel. Sticking an object in the barrel could alter or destroy telltale forensic marks.

On occasion, criminals try to obliterate or alter their own gun's markings by scratching or pouring acid into the barrel. That will work. It will change the markings enough to prevent the gun from being linked to a particular bullet. Some criminals also try to file down or scratch out a weapon's serial number, and most times that won't work. A crime lab can restore the number by using a chemical etching solution.

Incidentally, the correct way to collect a crime scene weapon is to put on cotton gloves and pick it up by the scored or rough surfaces—usually the grip, which won't hold prints anyway—and drop it into a clean bag.

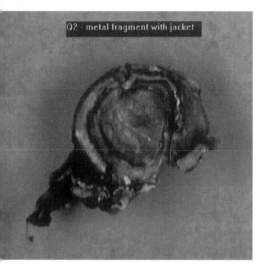

Q2 - metal fragment with jacket

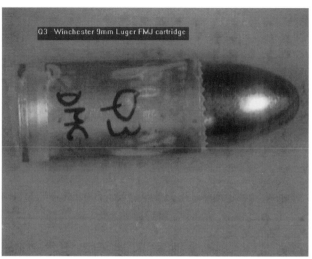

Q3 Winchester 9mm Luger FMJ cartridge

A smashed bullet alongside an unfired one. Even when a bullet is too damaged to be matched to a specific gun, it may carry valuable evidence in the form of particles of the material it has gone through.

cession at the same plant, will produce the same striations on a bullet. This is because minute imperfections on the moving tools used to cut rifled barrels produce unique striations on the inside of each barrel and because tiny chips of steel from the cutting process also get pressed into the barrel. The random distribution of these irregularities is impossible to reproduce. So when detectives are at the scene of a crime, they look for guns, bullets, and spent cartridge cases. If a suspect's gun is recovered, a lab technician fires test bullets from the gun into water. Then, with the aid of a comparison microscope, he or she compares the striations on the test bullets with the marks on the bullet from the crime scene to see if they match. Additionally, other machine-made parts of the weapon, such as the firing pin and the ejector, make contact with the cartridge case and imprint their own distinctive marks.

Other phenomena help to provide important clues. The examiner or technician can obtain information from *inside* the barrel. When a gun is fired, flame is emitted from the barrel, smoke follows the flame, and, as the bullet emerges from the barrel, more smoke and grains of both burned and unburned gunpowder follow it. A gunshot also produces a small but very powerful vacuum. If a gun is fired near anything soft, such as hair, or is fired through pillows or clothing, pieces of these materials may get sucked into the gun barrel in a phenomenon known as *blowback*. Police can use blow-back evidence to connect a gun with a crime scene. In one double-homicide case in Florida, a killer tried to muffle the sound of gunshots by shooting through a pillow. When the suspect was arrested, investigators found parts of a feather in his weapon's gun barrel. The particles were matched to the same feather pillow he had used at the crime scene to reduce the noise.

Because they hit things at high speed, bullets are usually damaged. Sometimes they are so flattened, smashed, or broken apart that they cannot be matched to a weapon. But there are situations when even that damage can be useful for investigators. When a bullet passes through something, it picks up and carries with it microscopic particles of that substance. Pieces of dirt, drywall, bone, or brick can be locked inside the smashed nose of a bullet and can help investigators figure out the bullet's path and, possibly, whether a victim was shot in the front or back.

The fact that residue, gas particles, and smoke are emitted from a gun along with the bullet enables investigators to ascertain a couple more things. Firearm and trace metal residue tests can tell us if someone has recently fired a gun, and more important, can be used to estimate the distance between the victim and the assailant.

When a weapon is fired, two metals found in the primer—barium and antimony—survive the burning process and often leave traces on the shooter's hand. There are several types of *gunshot residue test* (GSR) that can reveal the presence of these chemicals. In the

Bullets are sometimes difficult to find at a crime scene. FBI agents were involved in a shoot-out inside a house in St. Louis, Missouri. The suspect fired five shots. One bullet killed FBI agent Doug Adams, and two other agents were wounded. Four bullets were recovered, but the fifth, which had passed through an agent's leg, could not be found. After a week, investigators finally found the stray bullet in the kitchen sink, in six inches of water. Firearms examiners at the FBI lab determined from probing the bullet that it had passed through the agent's leg, gone through some indoor-outdoor carpet, hit the floor and bounced up through more carpet, struck a chair leg and deflected upward, bounced off the ceiling, and dropped into the sink.

Top: Gunshot residue particles under the extreme magnification of a scanning electron microscope. Bottom: Spectrum of gunshot residue showing the presence of barium (Ba), lead (Pb), and antimony (Sb).

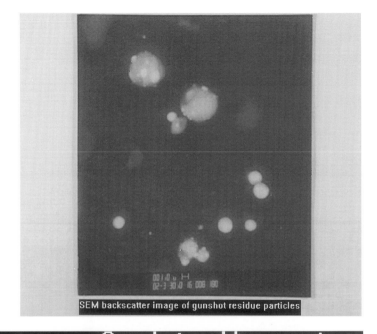

SEM backscatter image of gunshot residue particles

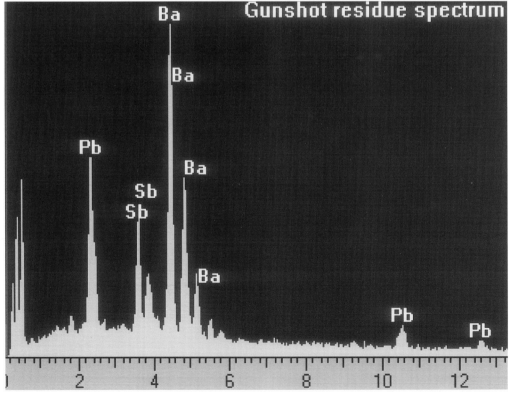

past, a "paraffin test" was used whereby warm liquid wax was poured over the suspect's hands, then peeled off and examined. Newer tests for the presence of residue now call for taking a series of cotton swabs dipped in dilute nitric acid solution and obtaining samples from the webbed area between the thumb and forefinger of the suspect. These tests can't necessarily establish that a suspect fired a gun but can refute claims that the suspect wasn't anywhere near a fired weapon.

Using a slightly different principle, investigators can help answer questions by testing for gunshot residue on the victim. When a bullet passes through any material, an invisible residue, mostly lead, is deposited around the bullet hole in a very specific pattern. When treated with chemicals that react to lead, the residue will leave a purple stain. The size or spread pattern varies according to the distance from the weapon to the victim. To illustrate, imagine that you were throwing a handful of black powder at a wall. The closer you were to the wall, the smaller the area the powder would cover; as you backed farther away, your powder pattern would grow larger. Logically, because the size of the pattern will be the same every time the same weapon is used with the same ammunition at the same distance, it's possible to figure out how far the shooter was from the victim by reproducing similar test conditions, thereby giving a distance marker. So when investigators find a compact residue pattern called *tattooing* or *stippling*—unburned powder or pieces of metal from the blast driven into the skin—they know this is the result of a close shot.

Like gunshot residues, fibers are small. A single thread is a fiber, as are all the tiny filaments that make up a thread. When fibers rub against something, they leave fragments of themselves on that thing. We might call fibers evidentiary minutiae, because some particles can be seen only through a microscope. Nevertheless, they can connect suspects to places or persons that they deny having had any contact with, helping to create a link between suspect, victim, and place. Fibers are extremely difficult to individualize to a specific source such as a sweater, pants, or a rug. Still, because fibers are transferred in such large numbers, they are much more likely to be found at a crime scene and are more likely to have a common origin. Ordinarily, after an examination of fiber evidence, a forensic microscopist will say, "They could have come from the same source."

Fibers are collected in several ways. If visible to the eye, they can be picked up with tweezers, or a section of material can be cut out and put into a clean bag. Sometimes they are picked up by taking wide cellophane tape and rolling it over the suspected area. Often the seats, floorboards, and trunk of a car are vacuumed for fiber particles when there is a suspected abduction or when probable cause indicates the transportation of a murder victim or some illegal product.

Pieces of fabric found at a crime scene can be examined in a manner similar to fibers to determine color, type of cloth and fiber, thread count, direction of fiber twist, and dye. When fabrics are torn or cut apart, the ends can be matched physically. In hit-and-run cases, pieces of the victim's clothing are often found on the grill, the car's fender, or the door handle. In addition, the differences between fabrics can be detected under a microscope, and a small tear in the clothing of a victim can be matched to another piece.

One particularly important case—the Atlanta child murders of 1979 to 1981—was solved almost entirely through physical evidence, mostly fibers. A series of greenish-yellow carpet fibers and other violet fibers were found on the bodies of many victims, on their clothes and in their hair. After much research, the fibers were painstakingly traced back to a carpet manufacturer in Dalton, Georgia. Luckily the Luxaire carpet identified, English Olive, had been discontinued after only one year in production. But before agents could track down all the buyers of this carpet, an Atlanta newspaper reported that police had found unique greenish-yellow fibers on the victims' fully clothed bodies. Soon after the news appeared, the killer began stripping his victims and dumping their bodies into the Chattahoochee River in an apparent attempt to wash away any hairs or fibers.

By the time the FBI crime lab became involved in the case in 1981, most of the murders had already been committed. But because the killer's pattern had changed, the Atlanta task force began staking out the bridges over the river. After Wayne Williams was caught dumping something into the river one night— and a body was later recovered downstream—police obtained warrants to search his home and vehicle. The greenish-yellow fibers matched the carpet in his home; the violet fibers, his bedspread.

It was still a tough case to prove in court "beyond a reasonable doubt." Eventually, though, with the aid of statistical evidence, including the presence of 27 fibers classified as unusual or uncommon, Wayne Williams's home was shown to be the environment shared by 12 murders. Although charged with only 2 of the 30 killings committed in a 22-month period, he was convicted of murder and sentenced to spend the rest of his life in prison.

Soil is just about everywhere—in yards, walkways, fields, parking lots, parks. And while all dirt might appear pretty much the same, in reality each soil sample is unique to a specific location. Consequently, soil can be valuable evidence. Soil differs from place to place because its constituent parts and the trace particles it contains—some naturally occurring, some human made—vary. Soil contains decayed or decaying organic matter, mostly from plants. Human activity, particularly near cities, also deposits paint particles, bits of concrete and asphalt, glass, airborne pollutants from factories, rubber from tire abrasion, and numerous other trace elements in the soil.

When a crime suspect is found with dirt in or on his clothes, shoes, or vehicle, a *forensic geologist* can determine whether the dirt came from a particular crime scene area.

In addition to its individual characteristics, soil also has useful class characteristics. As an investigative aid, an examination of an unknown soil sample by a forensic geologist may reveal the area from which the soil originated.

Additional clues about local conditions at the point of origin can be found by examining biological evidence. The presence of certain mosses, for example, may indicate a shaded area. A competent botanist can estimate the age of vegetation found under a body in

Blue-jean bar codes?

Blue jeans, a ubiquitous item of apparel worn by thousands of men, women, and children every day, are evidence of a relaxed fashion sensibility. Vorder Bruegge, however, wants us to consider them as evidence in an entirely new way: for the pattern along the leg seams that, Bruegge thinks, is as distinctive as a fingerprint.

In order to create the seams, the stitcher must guide thick layers of fabric under a needle, bit by bit. When the material is forced into folds, a variable pattern of ridges and valleys occurs quite naturally. As the jeans are washed and worn, the dye creates light and dark marks with irregular spacing and width. Bruegge sees a pattern resembling a bar code, something that can be mathematically matched.

In a case in Spokane, Washington, Bruegge demonstrated his findings in proceedings against a bank robber. The bank used a finely detailed 35-mm film in its surveillance camera and captured the pattern on the outside of the perpetrator's right pants leg. The overall collection of traits individual to a pair of his jeans—1 of 26 pairs collected from several suspects—matched the findings on the tape. During the trial, Bruegge said, "The bank robber depicted is wearing this pair of pants. I'm 100 percent certain."

The suspect was convicted. Although his verdict is on appeal, the prosecutor called Bruegge's blue-jeans testimony pivotal in winning the guilty verdict.

relation to foliage found in the immediate surrounding area. In one case, a skeleton found in wet Massachusetts ground had become intricately intertwined into a wild network of shrubs, weeds, and vines. The evidence was delivered to investigators in two huge blocks of earth. Although the delivery may have seemed a strange package, examiners were able to see the remains in the laboratory *in situ*—in the exact relation they had to the field. This was important because a careful study of the root system provided them with data on "time since death," because investigators could determine how many seasons had passed. Plus, when a root penetrates a bone, it keeps growing, and developing stems can ultimately break the bone into fragments, imitating other forms of trauma. Identifying the sites of bullet impact on the bones would have been impossible if investigators couldn't see where areas of similar destruction were due to later root growth.

One of the more famous cases solved using geology was the Coors murder case in Colorado. Beer company executive Adolph Coors III had been kidnapped on his way to work in 1961. His automobile was found on the road leading out of his ranch, but it was seven months before hunters found his body. A month after Coors disappeared, however, a car belonging to the prime suspect was found burned in a New Jersey dump. The fire had destroyed all the potential evidence *inside* the car, but investigators took soil samples from under the front fender. There were four different layers of dirt. The outer layer was soil from the dump, but the three other layers were matched with soil samples from the Rocky Mountain area. And one of those layers was matched to an area not far from the grave site. It was proof that the suspect had been in that area, and served as a key piece of evidence at the trial. Soil evidence helped to get a conviction for kidnapping and murder, and the suspect was sentenced to life in prison.

🐾   🐾   🐾

Just as matching soil samples can help solve a crime, so too can matching paint samples. The FBI has two crime laboratories, the Materials Analysis Unit and the Elemental Analysis Unit, that maintain a library of paint samples and other materials. One particularly large file is called the National Automotive Paint File. Started in 1932, it consists of more than 40,000 original paint finish samples. This tremendous stock of material enables examiners to identify the year, make, and model of any car by comparing the physical characteristics and chemical composition of paint found at a crime scene with that of known specimens. So although a few flakes of paint may not seem like much, in hit-and-run cases, they may make all the difference.

After a 10-year-old Los Angeles boy was killed by a hit-and-run driver, his clothes were sent to the lab. In an airtight scraping room examiners carefully rubbed paint off with a metal spatula. Tiny paint chips fell off the boy's pants; they had probably been pressed into the clothes by his blood and body fluids. The gold metallic paint identified was used on three model cars by the same manufacturer. The lab quickly notified the Los Angeles Police Department of its findings: the killer would be driving one of these models.

Soon after, police discovered that one of the boy's neighbors drove a gold sports car with a recently replaced hood. The suspect claimed the body work stemmed from a different traffic accident. To his dismay, however, the original hood was recovered, and the examiners not only matched the paint chips but also found fibers caught in the metal that matched the boy's jacket. Faced with this evidence, the owner of the car confessed to the crime.

In another case, a team of bank robbers in San Diego made the mistake of bumping into a parked car during their getaway. After the smudge was identified, the motor vehicle bureau helped by providing a list of

everyone in that area who owned that particular model. The foreign paint found on the parked car led directly to the apprehension of the bank robbers.

In addition to its collections of paint samples, the FBI has standards against which to test typewriting samples, watermarks, plastics and polymers, duct tape, gemstones, cosmetics, and even lubricants such as 85 types of petroleum jellies. Anything that can be used to build a bomb or aid in a crime is compared microscopically, microchemically, and instrumentally. All specimens must be identified using two different scientific methods, and following established protocols, before they can be used in court.

A forensic technician scrapes the jeans of a hit-and-run victim in an effort to obtain paint chips that may have been transferred from the car. Such paint would be traceable to a particular make and model because the FBI's National Automotive Paint File contains samples of every car paint finish.

♣   ♣   ♣

Glass is another common material. But there are many different kinds. Drinking glass is different from window glass, which is different from windshield glass or the lenses used in eyeglasses. And since glass is both durable and hard, even when shattered it can become embedded in, for example, a hammer, crowbar, or other tool used to break into a building. Plus, glass shards are almost impossible to clean up completely—they adhere invisibly to almost any surface.

Another interesting fact about glass is that even when a piece shatters into countless fragments, all of those fragments will have identical properties. Scientists find clues because the color, density, dispersion, and *refractive index* (the way light is bent when it travels through a substance other than air) will all be the same.

An illustrative case involved a serial rapist in Baltimore. One night the man broke into a woman's house but was confronted by her son. The intruder dove through a window to escape, but he was captured several blocks away. Not surprisingly, numerous slivers of glass were found on his body, in his clothing, and on his leather gloves.

When investigators examined the glass particles, they were initially puzzled. Some pieces of glass didn't match; they had apparently come from another location. The question was, where had these other pieces come from and how long had they been on the intruder's person? Baltimore police detectives decided to check unsolved rape cases in which the rapist had smashed windows to gain access. Sure enough, the glass evidence subsequently connected the intruder to three other rapes.

Scientists find answers in certain other violent crime investigations using glass studies. When bullets are fired through glass, three things can be determined: which side the shooter fired from, the angle from which the shot was fired, and the sequence in which multiple

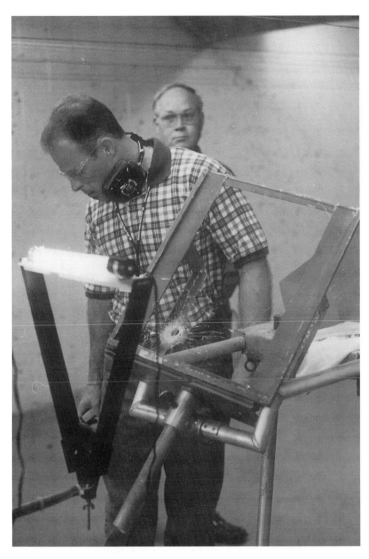

A criminalist examines ballistics equipment after test-firing a pistol. As the bullet passed through a line of three skyscreens (the triangular device), it cast a shadow that the skyscreens' photoelectric sensors detected, enabling the bullet's velocity to be calculated. The bullet then went through the pane of windshield glass and lodged in a block of "ballistics gelatin," which simulates the density of the human body. The test thus illustrates the bullet's penetration capabilities.

shots were fired. Intuitively we would think that when someone shoots through glass, the broken pieces will be found on the opposite side. That's not what happens, however. When glass breaks from applied force, it sprays back *toward the force*, not away from it. This is because glass is elastic; it bends, then snaps back violently, creating a phenomenon called blowback. In fact, blowback can throw particles as far as 18 feet in the direction from which the projectile came. From this, investigators can figure out how far away the shooter was standing by checking particles found on his or her clothes or on the ground.

In addition, it's possible to determine where a shot came from by looking at the type of angled hole the bullet left in the glass. And investigators can also learn from a sheet of glass the order in which shots were fired through it. Although shattering glass is a staple of movies and television cop shows, tempered glass or glass held secure by a frame will usually crack before it shatters. Several bullets are frequently required to shatter a pane of glass, and under certain circumstances the pattern of cracks can indicate the sequence of the shots.

♣   ♣   ♣

Many crimes—the vast majority, in fact—involve paper in some way. Obvious examples include crimes that are actually committed *on* paper, such as forgery, fraud, counterfeiting, and embezzlement. Other criminal activities—illegal gambling, smuggling, drug trafficking, prostitution—employ paper in record keeping. Paper plays a role in subtler forms of crime as well, like breach of contract, extortion, kidnapping, and suicide. And a criminal might use a credit card to buy supplies, sign a slip to rent a getaway car, get receipts for gun and ammunition purchases, sign a motel register, or endorse a check for an airline ticket. All of these activities leave a paper trail.

Forensic scientists can extract clues not only from what's written on a piece of paper but also from what's left behind as the result of manipulating paper and from the paper itself. The Document Section of the FBI's crime-science lab has seven different units responsible for investigating anything to do with paper: the machines used to create documents, the paper itself, the ink, anything that can't be seen with the naked eye, and sometimes even the meanings of words, numbers, or codes.

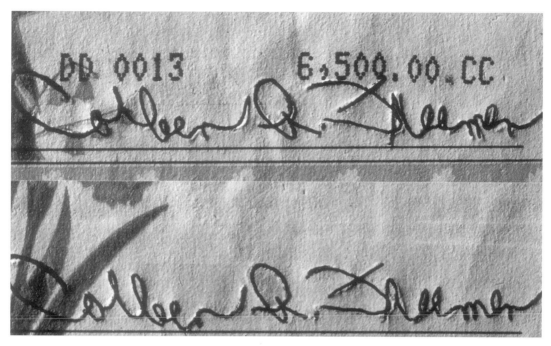

The basic philosophy behind document examination, or *questioned document examination*, is similar to that of other forms of physical evidence and evaluation. Investigators look for characteristics that vary from one sample to another, and the basic tools of the trade are a low-power microscope, a magnifying glass, and various light sources. Signature and handwriting constitute unique characteristics. Just as no two people share identical fingerprints, no two people write exactly the same way. Handwriting comparison is the most common type of document examination because forgery and fraud are as old as writing itself.

Distinction must be made between handwriting identification and handwriting analysis, or *graphology*. Handwriting identification, which is performed by *forensic linguists*, concentrates on the many factors that make up what is called "brain writing" (writing a person does habitually, without thinking about it), including the unconscious movements that make each person's writing unique and identifiable. There is no standard

Under low magnification, handwriting experts can compare a known sample with a questioned one and detect forgery.

A famous case that turned on handwriting comparison involved the eccentric billionaire Howard Hughes. After Hughes died in 1976, a previously unknown will surfaced at a Mormon church that bequeathed one-sixteenth of his estate to a gas station owner from Gibbs, Nevada, named Melvin Dummar. When reporters advised Dummar of his good fortune, he fainted. Although he couldn't say why Hughes, whom he didn't know, would have left him so much money, Dummar did recall having picked up an old man hitchhiking in the desert who had given him a document to be dropped off at a Mormon church. The reclusive Hughes did enough strange things in his later life that it seemed plausible he might abundantly reward someone for giving him a ride.

The FBI was called in to examine the case. The state of Nevada provided agent Jim Lile, a handwriting expert, with about 100 pages of Hughes's handwriting for comparison to the mysterious will. Lile said, "The first stroke of a pen on paper can either be tapered or blunt, but after that, most end strokes are tapered. The pen is moving when it leaves the paper and flows right into the next word. . . . If people do stop within a word, it's usually because they forgot how to spell it and pause to think about it. If there is any retouching, it's invariably for legibility. The Hughes will was full of those things I would expect to see in a simulated forgery. . . . It was a bad job." With the accumulation of this and other evidence, Dummar eventually confessed he'd made up the whole thing.

procedure for making a handwriting comparison. It boils down to experience in making side-by-side comparisons between known samples and the questioned document. By contrast, handwriting analysts, or graphologists, attempt to discern the personality traits and behavioral characteristics of the person who did the writing. For this, graphologists use elements in the writing, including things like slant, zone, upper and lower loop formulations, and any number of other repeated details that help to signal specific, potential behavioral features about the writer.

Everything about paper and writing can be tested. Writing instruments—pens, pencils, quills, paintbrushes, and so on—can be checked for class characteristics using visual inspection and stereomicroscopic examination. Occasionally, striation marks may appear in ballpoint pen writing and become an individual characteristic reflecting wear and tear on the instrument.

Paper can be tested for its chemical makeup, color, size, shape, watermarks, surface appearance, fluorescence, and any other properties aiding in identification. The dye used in colored papers can be identified by a technique called *thin-layer chromatography*. Other methods of chemistry can detect trace elements added to paper and can distinguish a paper's specialized fillers.

The pigment in ink remains on the surface of paper, but the solvent used to carry the pigment is absorbed into the fibers. While the visible part, the pigment, can be removed, the solvent will remain. Examiners can often make it visible by using different types of light and filters. Sometimes what cannot be seen by the eye can be picked up by cameras, which can be made to see through correction fluid or into a sealed envelope; sometimes they can even be used to read carbon traces on charred paper.

Other techniques such as the use of an *electrostatic detection apparatus* can enable examiners to pick up the impression of what was written on the paper underneath the original document. And a substance called *parylene* can give strength and resiliency to extremely brittle or crumpled material, allowing it to be opened, smoothed, and read.

Paper as trash has helped to solve countless crimes. When a Portland, Oregon, landlord cleaned out a house he had rented to a group of college-age individuals, a scrap of paper resembling a map drifted to the floor. It had an arrow designating a local bank that had recently been robbed. The landlord contacted authorities, and soon FBI agents were sifting through trash and a dumpster near the house. After seven weeks of searching and putting together thousands of tiny scraps of paper, agents had enough fingerprints and evidence to arrest eight people in connection with a variety of crimes, including four other bank robberies, the planned kidnapping of the mayor of Portland, and the attempted bombing of an army induction center.

You never know what's in the trash that may help to solve a crime. Trash to some, treasure to others.

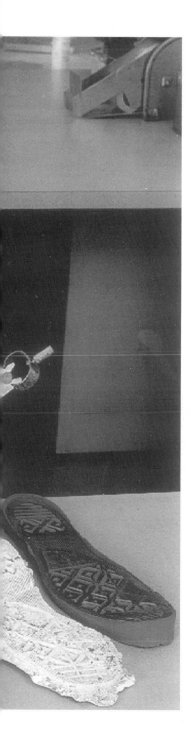

IMPRESSIONS EVIDENCE

I t's hard to commit a crime without your hands. And hands readily leave behind impressions that forensic technicians and scientists can recover. Fingerprints and palm prints, unique characteristics of every human being, are among the most important impressions evidence in the investigation of crime.

If you look at the underside of your fingers in a strong light, you'll see a number of tiny ridges in the skin. These are called *friction ridges*. Notice that the ridges aren't all connected; they create patterns where they peak, curve, and divide. These patterns are what make your fingerprints unique and identifiable. And, unlike the many organic changes that take place in the

An FBI expert compares sneaker treads with plaster castings of foot-prints. A casting can be used to identify such characteristics as the shoe's manufacturer and its size. In addition, unique patterns of wear can sometimes show that a particular shoe made a given crime-scene footprint.

body over the course of a lifetime, the arrangement of these friction ridges was fixed about four months before birth and will never vary. If, for some reason, the skin is ever removed, the ridges will grow back in the same pattern.

Beneath the epidermis, the outer layer of the skin, lie billions of microscopic sweat and sebaceous, or oil, glands. The perspiration and body oils these glands secrete reach the surface of the skin through tiny openings called pores. Perspiration, or sweat, is 98.5 percent water, but the other 1.5 percent—composed of dissolved salt, amino acids, proteins, and other chemicals—is left behind on the skin after evaporation. Skin oil helps this and other residue and dirt adhere. When a person touches certain objects or surfaces, some of the oil and dirt in fingerprint ridges is transferred to the object or surface, leaving a print. Even clean hands have enough natural oils to transmit faint fingerprints. And hands that have touched such materials as grease, oil, cosmetics, or fatty foods like potato chips readily leave fingerprint impressions.

The history of fingerprints for identification is as old as the T'ang dynasty, which ruled China from A.D. 618 to 906. During this period, official divorce documents and most business contracts required a man's thumbprint. Fourteenth-century Persia also used fingerprints on government documents. In the late 1600s, a member of the British Royal Society of Physicians published a lecture in which he discussed ridge patterns on the fingertips, but it wasn't until 1858 that fingerprinting for identification was first used by a Western society. In that year, Sir William Herschel, the British administrator of a large district in India, began requiring Indian subjects to seal contracts with fingerprints in addition to their signatures.

Dactyloscopy—the scientific study of fingerprints—arose in response to law enforcement's need to identify convicts. In earlier civilizations, criminals were some-

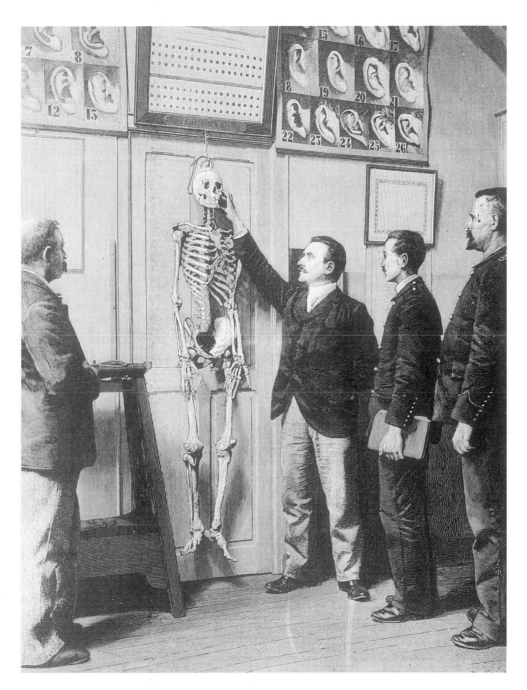

French policemen being instructed in the Bertillon system. The system, developed in 1879, offered a way to identify convicted criminals by taking a series of precise measurements of various bony body parts. No two people, it was believed, shared the exact same Bertillon measurements.

times tattooed or had their fingers or a hand cut off to differentiate them from the law-abiding. In the early 1800s, the notion that policemen should memorize convicts' faces for the future was common. Growing crime rates made that somewhat impractical, however. In 1879 a French criminologist named Alphonse Bertillon came up with a method of identifying people based on measurements of bony parts of the body. Using up to 14 different measurements—including the circumference of the head, the length and width of the right ear, the length and width of the left middle and little fingers, and the length of the left forearm and foot—the Bertillon system produced high odds against two people having the exact same measurements. Nearly every nation used the system until the early 20th century.

In 1903, however, authorities got a shock. A convict named Will West found his near double, a second criminal whose name, coincidentally, was William West, at Fort Leavenworth Prison. The men had essentially the same Bertillon measurements and looked like identical twins. The only thing that distinguished them was the difference in their fingerprints. The coincidence helped spur the creation of a national fingerprint bureau and the establishment, by Congress, of a national repository of fingerprint records in 1924.

Today the Identification Division of the FBI has more than 200 million prints representing more than 68 million people. About 70 percent of all people arrested already have their prints on file somewhere in the Criminal Justice Information Services Division. The method for taking fingerprints is still pretty much the same as it has always been. Printer's ink is spread on a glass plate with a roller, and the person to be fingerprinted has his fingers rolled one at a time through the ink and then pressed on a card. Full handprints, called flat prints, are then taken to ensure that each finger is assigned the correct numbered position. Computer fingerprint copiers are less messy and allow the image to be logged directly into the database along with the suspect's file information and photograph.

For crime scene investigators, the first problem with fingerprints is knowing where to look for them and how to develop them. Experienced examiners will start with the criminal's points of entry and exit. Then they look to what's been disturbed or manipulated. Things like door handles, telephones, windows, glasses, and light switches are checked, with special attention given to objects that may have caused obvious damage. In a particular federal case, bank robbers had taken the time to carefully wipe down every inch of an apartment they'd lived in for weeks. On their departure, though, someone had forgotten to turn on the dishwasher, and all kinds of prints were taken off plates, glassware, and silverware.

Detectives look for three different types of fingerprints at crime scenes:

- *Plastic prints* are those that leave an impression in soft, pliable surfaces—for example, putty, gum, new paint, wax, flour, soap, grease, or tar. A negative impression of the friction ridge pattern is produced in the substance.
- *Visible prints* happen when fingers contaminated by dust, ink, blood, grease, face powders, oils, or a hundred other materials touch a clean surface, leaving a print that can be readily seen.
- *Latent prints* are invisible. These are the fingerprints formed from perspiration and oils. They are found on objects with smooth or polished surfaces or on paper. Latent prints are developed by either a dusting or chemical process or both.

There are at least 40 ways to develop fingerprints. The most common and practical method is the dusting technique. A fine dusting powder is lightly brushed over the surface bearing prints. A different color of powder is used depending on the color of the object to

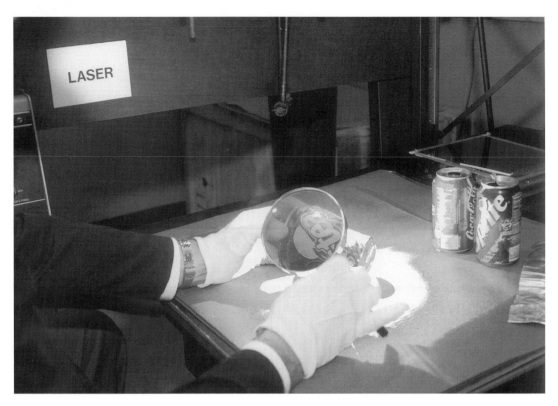

Lasers are a valuable tool for finding fingerprints. Not only do they not destroy the print, but they also are effective with older evidence.

be dusted. If the object is dark, a light powder is used; if it is light or white, a black powder is used. Most latent prints will first appear as a smudge. Further, delicate brushing parallel to the ridge structure with a soft brush will bring the print out. The print is then photographed using a special camera, after which it is "lifted." To lift a print, the technician places a clear, sticky tape over it, then carefully removes the tape, which now holds the fingerprint, and places it on an index card along with other pertinent information.

Chemical methods of fingerprint preservation include iodine fuming, use of ninhydrin or silver nitrate, and fuming with Super Glue. In iodine fuming, the oldest chemical method, iodine crystals are heated, transforming them into vapor. Some experts believe that the iodine vapors combine with the fatty oils in latent prints; others think that the iodine may actually interact with residual water left on a print from perspiration. Ninhydrin, which is commonly sprayed onto porous surfaces from aerosol cans, reacts chemically with the amino acids present in perspiration to form a purple-blue print. Silver nitrate, frequently used to develop fingerprints on paper or cardboard, reacts to the salt present in perspiration to form silver chloride. Though silver chloride is itself colorless, exposure to ultraviolet light will develop a black or reddish-brown print. Super Glue fuming works best on nonporous surfaces such as metals, electrical tape, leather, and plastic bags; it also sometimes brings out prints on a victim's body. A tent is created around the object and then Super Glue, which is mainly cyanocrylate ester, is heated. The fumes adhere to the moisture found in latent prints and form hard, white, visible ridges. If investigators want to try all of the above development methods on the same surface, they must use iodine fuming first, followed by ninhydrin, then silver nitrate, then Super Glue fuming.

Lasers—high-energy light sources—provide a nonchemical method of finding fingerprints. No one knows why lasers make some prints visible when the other techniques fail, but they seem to work better on older evidence. They have the advantage of not damaging the evidence, but their high cost often puts them out of the reach of small jurisdictions. For these jurisdictions, alternative light sources (ALSs) are often the answer. For example, RAM, a fluorescent dye, causes some prints to show under ultraviolet light. In a dark room, a high-intensity arc light with special filters makes latent prints glow like magic.

Finding a print, however, is just the beginning. Without the name of a suspect or at least a lead, it could be extremely difficult to find a match among the millions of prints on file. Until the 1980s the process of fingerprint identification was tedious, time-consuming, and, in most cases, overwhelming. Police would search through regular file cabinets of samples.

There are three main fingerprint types: arches, loops, and whorls. These are subdivided into plain arches and tented arches; radial loops and ulnar loops; plain whorls, double loop whorls, central pocket loop whorls, and accidentals. Plus, the classifications and system methods are varied. Not only that, but perpetrators rarely leave prints of all 10 fingers at a crime scene. So basically, there are 10 times as many single prints as there are sets of prints, and often it is impossible to tell just which finger left its mark.

The computerization of prints has been one of the keys to laying open the fingerprint file. In fact, when the first computer system for fingerprints, the Automated Fingerprint Identification System (AFIS), went on-line, some older cases were cleared off the books. In 1990, for example, the Los Angeles Police Department entered fingerprints obtained at the scene of about 50 unsolved homicide cases dating back to the 1960s. (The statute of limitations would have run out on anything but murder, so there was no point in matching prints from other crimes.)

One particularly interesting case dealt with the brutal beating and strangulation of a 43-year-old waitress named Thora Marie Rose in 1963. Rose had been found in her apartment; she'd been beaten with a claw hammer and strangled with a silk stocking. Investigators knew she had spent the evening before her death dancing at the Continental Hotel in Hollywood and had returned to her apartment around midnight. The perpetrator entered sometime after, gaining entrance by removing glass louvers from a window at the rear.

The fingerprint expert who examined the crime scene had lifted 35 prints from the louvers, the kitchen sink, and the bedroom walls, among other places. When he first matched them, he discovered that he had all five fingers from the killer's right hand and four prints from the left.

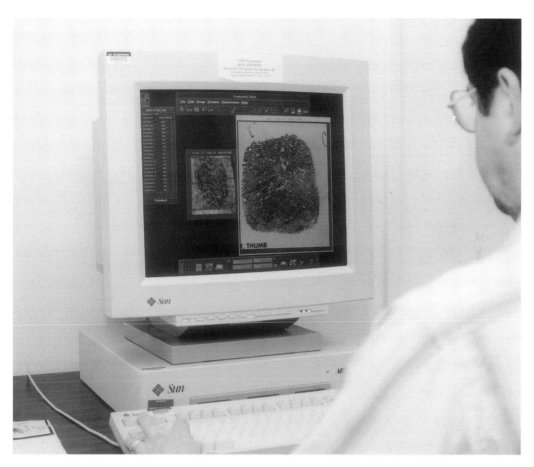

The computer did what would have taken analysts years. Certain commands narrowed down the parameters and then hunted through millions of remaining prints on-line. Eventually it found a match. Vernon Robinson, a resident of Minneapolis, Minnesota, had been a navy recruit stationed in San Diego at the time of Rose's death. Now he was a $70,000-a-year executive. Although he denied any knowledge of the murder, when the latent prints were compared with new prints taken from Robinson, they were found to be an exact match. In 1993 Vernon Robinson was convicted of the 30-year-old murder and sentenced to life in prison.

While criminals may go to great lengths to avoid leaving fingerprints at a crime scene, they may care-

An expert compares fingerprints on-screen through the FBI's Automated Fingerprint Identification System (AFIS). AFIS has revolutionized the process of fingerprint identification, which had previously required that law enforcement manually search through thousands or even millions of fingerprint files to find a match with prints from a crime scene. Now computers do the searching.

Even evidence as fragile as footprints in dust can provide forensic investigators with important clues. This photo shows a footwear tread impression after a lifting powder has been applied. Next an electrostatic dust lifter will be used to preserve the impression. The writing at the top left is to show that the photo isn't a negative.

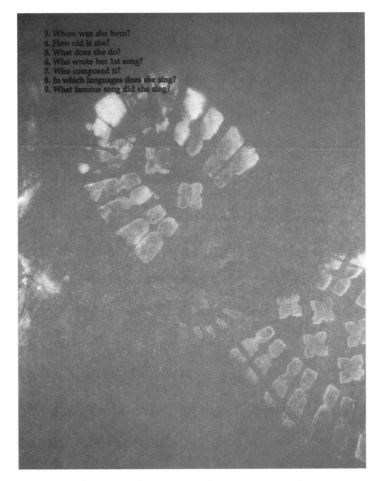

3. Where was she born?
4. How old is she?
5. What does she do?
6. Who wrote her 1st song?
7. Who composed it?
8. In which languages does she sing?
9. What famous song did she sing?

lessly neglect another area of impression, shoe prints. The footprint is the most common impression left at or near a crime scene. Prints are found outside in dirt, mud, clay, loam, and snow. In urban areas they may be found on the rooftops of apartment buildings. Occasionally they are found inside houses, when perpetrators have tracked dirt in or when they have tracked through something that will hold a print, such as paint or blood.

Shoe types and styles number in the thousands. For that reason, comparisons are first narrowed down by class characteristics: size, type, brand, design, shape. Next comes an examination of the individual characteristics: nicks, scratches, or cuts from wear patterns, perhaps a pebble wedged into the tread. Even with deck shoes (rubber-soled loafers), the stitching in the soles is done randomly, and no two will be identical in relief. Although matching a footprint with a suspect's shoes doesn't in itself establish that he or she committed the crime, it does mean that the suspect will need a good explanation for his or her presence at the crime scene.

The first step for investigators who find footwear or tire impressions at a crime scene is to photograph the imprints. If they've left a depression in mud, for example, a cast, or *moulage*, is then made. To do this the investigator will clean out any loose material without disturbing the impression. Next, a fixative is sprayed onto the surface. Then a portable frame or wood ledge is built around the track. Plaster or dental stone casting material is poured over the marks. Reinforcement sticks or cheesecloth is placed into the mixture as it hardens. When hardened, the casting is carefully lifted and put into a cardboard box upside down to dry. Another product, Snow Print Wax, can be used for impressions found in packed snow.

In addition to serving as a possible aid in identifying someone at a crime scene, casts can provide clues as to the person's movements. The cast of a person who is running, for example, will show a deeper impression at the front of the foot with less weight distributed to the heel. Whether the person was carrying something heavy, was wounded, or carried off soil samples on his or her shoes can also be determined.

Like latent fingerprints, shoe prints that aren't visible can be lifted from countertops, staircases, and walls through the use of chemicals and powder. But for the flimsiest of all evidence, shoe prints found in dust, another system is needed. The best way to find these is to turn out the lights and shine an oblique light—a flashlight will do—against the hard, dusty surface. But the best method to preserve such prints is to use an electrostatic dust lifter. This device works by spreading a sheet of black lifting material, like foil, over the surface. When a high-voltage charge is run through the material, the electricity makes the print stick to the lifter. The process is nondestructive and works on just about any surface. One bank robber who had walked over the counter during a holdup found his shoes matched to the print taken from the surface using this method.

Actually, the principle behind this ingenious instrument for detection was discovered quite by accident. A Japanese policeman who did television repair as a sideline found that dust was attracted to the high-voltage source in the back of the TV set and realized that this property could be adapted for crime-solving. A case of serendipity rendered useful.

Tire tread evidence is governed by the same principles as footprint evidence, and more than one criminal has been matched to a crime by the tires on his or her car. Sometimes hit-and-run victims also bear tire mark evidence, but not in a way one might expect. As a car runs over a body, the victim's clothing can wrap around the tires, imprinting the sidewall, where the brand name and number appears, on the cloth. Several court cases have been aided by this phenomenon.

♠   ♠   ♠

Toolmarks also have stories to tell. With sufficient pressure, tools leave scratches and impressions in softer materials, and the marks they create stay behind to tell the tale. Much can be learned about a violation and its methodology from careful examination of toolmarks.

Almost every crime involves some kind of tool. Shovels move dirt when evidence is buried, crowbars are handy for breaking doorjambs, screwdrivers sometimes force open windows, pliers help make bombs, and wire cutters clip through fences. The tools involved in these procedures make scars, scrapes, dents, chips, and grooves, and these marks can be traced back to the source, just like striation marks on bullets or the friction ridges on fingertips.

Police often look for toolmarks at a crime scene. Then, when a suspect is identified, they get a search warrant for his or her home or car and try to match any found tool with its marks, because every tool is unique. No matter how well a tool is forged and polished, it has microscopic defects or marks on its striking or cutting surface. Plus, hard employment can produce slight chips or faults. A crime-scene object bearing a toolmark is therefore photographed and, if movable, submitted to the lab. It's not uncommon for investigators to saw off pieces of doorjamb, turn in small safes and locked drawers, or bring in bits of metal that may have come from the tip of a knife or the claw-side end of a hammer.

Essentially, the way to conduct a toolmark examination and comparison is to produce marks on a surface similar to the one bearing the evidence, using the tool in question. The two sets of marks are then compared microscopically.

Tools can also be a source of trace evidence, carrying on them tiny pieces of hair, fibers, paint, or soil. And toolmark examiners can make *fracture matches*— matching a small broken fragment to the tool from which it came. A case from Virginia illustrates this technique. A series of robberies of bank night-deposit boxes were committed using hammers, crowbars, and screwdrivers. The method of removing the boxes was pretty clear, but since that was all detectives had to go on, the investigation stalled. One night, however, an investigator found a tiny piece of broken metal at the scene of one of the robberies, which police held onto as a clue. Later, when several suspects were identified and search warrants were obtained, police found various broken screwdrivers among the suspects' possessions. The broken metal tip recovered and saved from the one crime scene told examiners its tale. The piece matched perfectly one of the broken screwdrivers found in the suspects' possession, and the toolmark evidence was enough to put the gang away.

Remember, too, that teeth are tools, and criminals sometimes use their teeth when committing a crime. And many victims, particularly small children, bite their attackers in self-defense. Bite-mark evidence can have particular value in the investigation of sexual assaults. Theodore Robert "Ted" Bundy, one of America's most notorious serial murderers, was eventually convicted because of such evidence. In 1978 he had murdered two female students at Florida State University, leaving bite marks on one of the victims. After his arrest, police took a wax impression of his teeth, and at trial a forensic odontologist superimposed an enlarged photograph of the impression over an enlarged photograph of the victim's wound. They matched "almost like a key fitting in a lock," and the jury convicted Bundy. In 1989 he was executed in Florida's electric chair.

Dr. Norman "Skip" Sperber, chief forensic dentist for San Diego and Imperial counties in California, had a rather unusual case involving bite marks. A man had forced a 16-year-old girl into his pickup truck and driven her to a secluded grove. While her kidnapper wasn't looking, the girl made a smart move. Standing outside the truck, she bit the weather stripping on one of the doors in the hopes of leaving evidence behind.

Police eventually arrested the kidnapper, but he had sold his truck, and the authorities didn't locate it until just days before the trial. When called in to identify the vehicle, the girl remembered biting the soft rubber and pointed out the mark to investigators.

Dr. Sperber entered the picture then, almost two years after the crime. He examined the yard-long piece of weather stripping, and sure enough, he recognized the four tiny rectangular marks as the impressions left

by four lower teeth. One of the tooth marks was slightly out of line with the others, a key clue for any competent forensic dentist.

Sperber later demonstrated the match evidence to a jury, which convicted the suspect. The verdict of the case is on appeal, but the bite-mark impressions Sperber recovered from the weather stripping were never under question.

While even a layperson can see rough similarities in bite marks and teeth, the forensic odontologist uses an array of equipment, including infrared and ultraviolet photography, electron microscopy, computer analysis, and plaster casts of the suspect's teeth to make precise comparisons. The size and shape of the teeth are studied, as are any crooked, jagged, or missing teeth; ridges;

A dowel inserted through a bullet hole in glass can tell investigators the angle from which the shot was fired. Note that even though this windshield has been pierced by more than 10 bullets, it hasn't shattered. The pattern of cracks can reveal the sequence of the shots.

fillings; and chips, grooves, and spaces between teeth, along with other imperfections. Even people with perfect teeth have a distinctive bite. A Texas case was solved more than 40 years ago because of bite evidence. Before leaving a grocery store he had robbed, a man took a bite out of a piece of cheese. Investigators later matched the bite marks to the suspect, proving that the rat gets the cheese (and jail) in the end.

Few of the units involved in lab work ever visit a crime scene, and only rarely do they see a body. The on-site reconstruction of crime scene scenarios usually has something to do with bullets and the residue associated with guns. For example, *trajectory analysis*—determining the path the bullet traveled from its angle of impact—can answer a lot of reconstruction questions crucial to establishing the position of the shooter. In some cases, determination of the trajectory will lead to the immediate recovery of a bullet.

For short trajectories, investigators often insert probes, such as metal or wooden dowels, into bullet holes. When probes are impractical because of the long distances involved, string or twine is used. Over very long distances, string will sag, so a small, low-power laser is lit behind some fog or smoke to create an overall visualization and for photographic documentation of the trajectory.

Distance determination generally involves identifying gunshot residue and the interpretation of shot and powder patterns, but blood splatterings can also help investigators zero in on distance and other factors. From studying blood splatters on walls and floors, for example, experts can determine where an assault took place, the direction of the blows, and the amount of force used. They look at spot size, shape and distribution of blood, angle of impact, and quantity of blood. The appearance of a drop of blood that has landed on a surface will vary according to the height from which it fell and the texture of the surface. In a short fall onto a smooth, flat surface, the drop will be round. Jagged edges will appear as the height is increased. Other unique conditions exist if the person from whom the blood came is in motion, or if a club was used to bludgeon the victim. Entire books have been written about *bloodstain pattern evidence*, and it is an extremely valuable and interesting specialty.

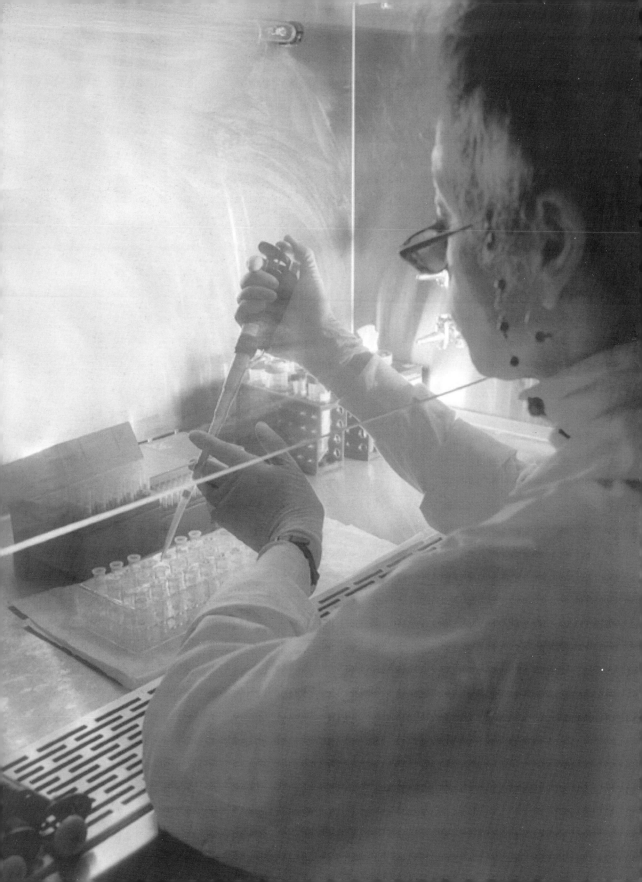

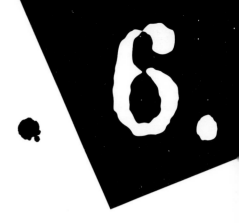

HIGH-TECH TOOLS

A technician prepares samples for polymerase chain reaction, a technique that allows large amounts of DNA to be synthesized from a small sample. This, in turn, will make it possible to run a number of DNA tests. DNA fingerprinting, a powerful tool that enables investigators to match suspects with a crime scene through any biological material left behind, was first used in a criminal trial in 1987.

The technology of forensic science continually advances. Tools and techniques that were unknown 50, or even 20 or 25, years ago are now routinely used to solve crimes. Some labs now have special microscopes that can magnify particles found at a crime scene by up to 200,000 times. Sophisticated machines and new procedures help scientists identify even trace chemicals found in complex mixtures. A single drop of blood can establish the identity of a suspect with the certainty of a fingerprint.

But while the technology of forensic science has changed dramatically, one thing hasn't changed: the importance of the investigator. For more than just familiarity with the latest high-tech tools is required from the men and women who probe crime. They must have the ability to look at *all* the pieces of a puzzle, to utilize careful questioning and keen analysis. Because each crime is unique, they must be able to bring a fresh perspective to the task at hand, to be willing to learn anew. Without that, all the technology in the world won't get to the bottom of a complicated crime.

To take a simple example, most of us think that all blood is red or, when it dries, black. The experienced investigator knows that large amounts of blood exposed to the air for hours can indeed turn a glossy black, dry in layers, and crack. But, depending on the surface blood falls on, it may appear brown, pink, or even greenish in hue.

Perpetrators often try to clean up the blood trail of a crime, assuming that if they wash down the walls and floor, no one will be able to see the traces. A good investigator armed with clues and an instinct for further investigation, however, won't assume that a floor that appears immaculate to the naked eye has no blood on it. The investigator will spray the suspicious area with a chemical called Luminal and turn out the lights. Any traces of blood will glow fluorescent, outlining further evidence of the crime. And oddly enough, the older the blood, sometimes the better the sign.

But Luminal isn't especially high-tech; it's just a reagent that produces the right result. The use of computers and special software programs, on the other hand, represents a quantum leap in the way forensic scientists do their work. Computers enable investigators to

- access more information more quickly
- store countless bits of data for retrieval from literally anywhere
- aid in fingerprint identification and DNA fingerprinting
- produce face re-creations
- enhance and manipulate video images.

We'll talk about some of those things here.

The criminal justice system generates mind-boggling quantities of records and documents. In the past, all had to be committed to paper. Computers have boosted

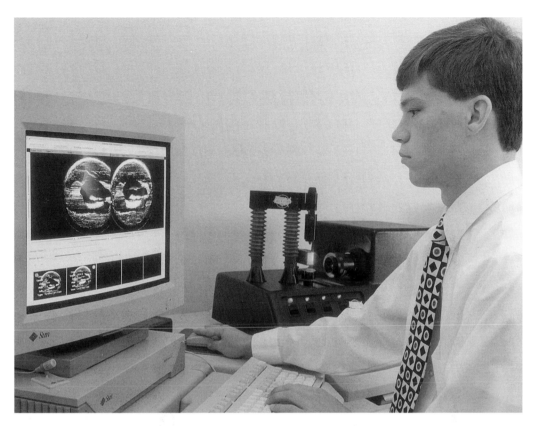

the efficiency and effectiveness of police and forensic operations enormously by greatly simplifying record keeping and information retrieval. They enable police to research a suspect with a few keystrokes. Uniformed officers can access the computer in their patrol cars to find out whether a vehicle has been reported stolen, to run a driver's license number for a record of any infractions, and to process fingerprints in order to check a person's records. An extension program is available for missing persons, firearms, and stolen property, plus information on the public's most wanted, with data available on people considered dangerous to the government and even to the president.

The FBI's National Crime Information Center (NCIC) is a huge computerized database that allows law-enforcement agencies nationwide to share infor-

An operator at a Drugfire workstation does a side-by-side comparison of ballistics evidence from two different cases. Drugfire, an FBI program, was conceived as a way to allow investigators around the country to link drug-related shootings in different jurisdictions. It has since expanded to include ballistics evidence from all crimes in which a gun is fired.

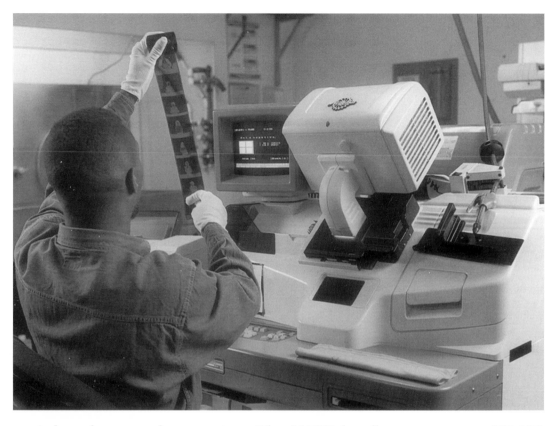

A photo-enhancement technician examines a roll of negatives. He'll use the computer to digitize the images, which will then be divided into tiny squares called pixels. By adjusting the color saturation pixel by pixel, the computer can clear up hazy images.

mation. The NCIC handles as many as 750,000 inquiries each day, and quite quickly. It has also built bridges between different jurisdictions. Years ago, if a weapon was used in a murder in St. Louis, for example, there was no way to check its characteristics with ballistics evidence from a murder in Kansas City. Since 1992, though, a program called Drugfire, initiated by the FBI Firearms Unit, has enabled departments to associate gun killings. A new computer process has made it possible to create a digital image of the marks on the surface of a cartridge case, and to characterize them in terms of numbers. When two digital images match in number, they can be transmitted to different crime labs for comparison, whereupon a physical evidence examination will ensue. Drugfire was originally supposed to connect only drug-related shootings, but it has expanded to include all crimes in which a weapon is fired.

Computers also facilitate the development of photographs. When pictures from a bank's surveillance camera catch a bank robber on film, a computerized digital image-processing procedure called photo enhancement, or image enhancement, can bring a face into focus out of a hazy background. One case involved a murderer in Cayce, South Carolina, who routinely made withdrawals with his victim's automatic teller machine (ATM) card. Officials recovered a surveillance camera photo from one of the banks where the killer had made an ATM withdrawal. Unfortunately, the photo had been taken in poor light, on old film, by an antiquated camera. In fact, the image was so dark that authorities weren't even sure there was a figure on the film, but they submitted it to the FBI lab for enhancement.

To enhance a photograph, the computer divides an image into *pixels*, tiny squares of picture elements. Each square is a shade of gray and is measured on a scale from 0 (pure black) to 250 (pure white). The human eye can't even detect the difference between some of the gray-scale squares that the computer makes lighter or darker, creating a contrast in order to help the image appear separate from its background. The resulting image may appear grainy, but it can still be useful. The Cayce suspect, for example, confessed when he saw the enhanced image the FBI produced from the ATM film.

These days, as camcorder use increases, so do the odds that a crime committed in a public area will be serendipitously recorded, providing powerful evidence for police investigations. An HBO documentary titled *Autopsy 5: Dead Men Do Tell Tales* relates such a story. An amateur videographer captured on tape an assailant strangling to death a man named David Adder. The tape also showed the killer taking cigarettes from the victim's pocket before fleeing. Police apprehended a suspect, Cheryl Metcalf, for the killing. Fortunately for Metcalf, she had a unique identifiable marker: she was missing three of the fingertips from her left hand. With the aid of video enhancement, researchers were able to inform the police that the woman in the video—the real killer—had intact all five fingers on her left hand. Her innocence thus established, Metcalf was released. The killer remained at large.

One of the more startling video-related cases is the 1991 murder of Constable Darrell Lunsford in Garrison, Texas. After the courts released a drug-smuggling suspect he had apprehended for lack of evidence, Lunsford decided to mount a video camera on the dashboard of his patrol car. One night, after he had stopped a motorist for reckless driving, the camera captured the final moments of Lunsford's life. The tape showed the constable, illuminated by the headlights of his patrol car, starting to open the trunk of the car he had stopped. Suddenly, three men jumped out of the car, grabbed his gun, pushed him into a ditch, and shot him in the head. When his body was found, the video camera was still running.

Although the three killers couldn't be seen distinctly, the tape enabled police to develop general descriptions, and the men were arrested shortly thereafter. Meanwhile, a duplicate tape had been sent to a lab for enhancement. At the trial, although little other evidence was presented, the jury was able to identify the men on the enhanced tape. The suspects were convicted of the murder of Constable Lunsford.

We've talked about the many ways criminals can be identified and how forensic evidence can pile up against them. A fairly new technology provides forensic scientists with a statistically undeniable identification at its most basic level—that of an individual cell. The technology is commonly referred to as *DNA fingerprinting*.

DNA, *deoxyribonucleic acid*, is a large, complex, two-stranded molecule found in the nuclei of living cells. In structure, it resembles two spiral strands that wrap around each other and are bound together by runglike sections; it is therefore sometimes referred to as the *double helix*. Each strand of the molecule comprises a long chain of *nucleotides*, chemical compounds made up of three basic parts: a phosphate, a sugar, and one of four bases. These four bases are adenine (A), cytosine (C), guanine (G), and thymine (T). Each DNA strand is arranged in an order complementary to the other. A strand with a base sequence A-G-C-T, for example, will bind to a T-C-G-A strand sequence (adenine always pairs with thymine, cytosine with guanine).

DNA has an essential function: it provides the genetic code passed on from parent to offspring, the code that determines the structure, characteristics, and development of all cellular organisms—plant or animal. It's what makes a daffodil differ from a duck and a duck differ from a human. It's also what makes one person's eyes blue and another's brown. The code itself resides in the sequence of the "letters," the bases A, T, C, and G.

All genetically normal humans have 46 chromosomes, half inherited from each parent. The chromosomes carry our genes, segments of DNA that consist of a specific sequence of letters controlling production of a particular protein. Researchers believe that the entire human genetic code, or genome, consists of 80,000 to 100,000 individual genes and about three billion separate nucleotide letters, the genes' building blocks.

Because we all share tens of thousands of genes, which are located at specific areas of specific chromosomes, we all share many genetically determined characteristics. To take but a few large and visible examples, everyone has hands, ears, a nose, eyes, and skin. But because no two people—except identical twins—have *exactly* the same letter sequence in their DNA, humans appear, and are, quite diverse. To confirm this we need only look at a few people carefully, and we'll discern differences in size and shape of hands, ears, and nose; differences in shape and color of eyes; and differences in skin color. In the human genome's three-billion-letter sequence, there are about 10 million spots where the letters can vary from person to person, giving each of us our unique characteristics. Segments of DNA that vary are called *polymorphic segments* or *genetic markers*.

Although the molecular structure of DNA was discovered in 1953, more than 30 years passed before forensic applications became available. In 1984 an English scientist named Dr. Alec Jeffreys, who was studying how genes evolve, developed an aid to mapping genetic markers. Jeffreys's procedure yielded an X ray that showed light and dark bands of variable widths, like a bar code. Jeffreys was astonished at both the detail and individual specificity of the genetic bar codes; each person's varied noticeably. Thus the procedure came to be called "genetic fingerprinting" or "DNA fingerprinting." In the process of further testing his discovery, Jeffreys stumbled onto a key fact that would have profound implications for forensic science: every cell in a person's body contains the same DNA and will therefore yield the same DNA fingerprint. That means that even very tiny amounts of blood, semen, vaginal fluid, saliva, perspiration, urine—even hair root—all can be used to identify a criminal suspect.

In simple terms, here is how DNA fingerprinting is done (using a technique called restriction fragment length polymorphisms, or RFLP):

- A blood sample is taken from a suspect.
- White blood cells are removed from the blood sample and one white cell is burst open to release its DNA strands.
- The DNA is then mixed with a special enzyme, called a restriction enzyme, that cuts the DNA

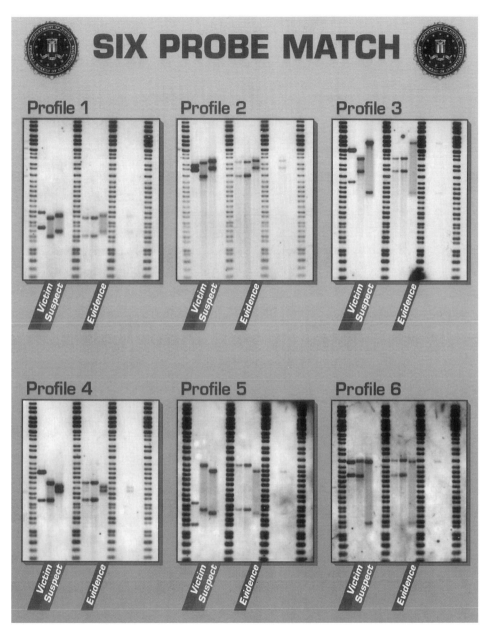

DNA results from a rape case, showing the victim's and the suspect's profiles compared with the evidence. Note that in each of the six probes, the dark bands of the suspect's sample align perfectly with dark bands from the evidence sample. (The bands represent polymorphic segments of DNA to which the radioactive probes have attached.) The semen collected after the crime, therefore, almost certainly came from the suspect.

at specific sites (for example, anywhere an A-C-C-G-T-A sequence occurs). The restriction fragments will vary in length, with some containing polymorphic segments.

- The fragments are placed on a sheet containing a special gel, and an electric current is then applied to the gel by means of electrodes. This technique is called electrophoresis.
- Under electrophoresis, the DNA fragments move toward the positive electrode. The shorter fragments move more quickly than do the longer fragments, and after a time, the fragments have all lined up according to size.
- The new formation is transferred to a nylon membrane called a *blot*.
- The blot is exposed to a genetic *probe*. That is, a particular type of DNA molecule, or probe, is applied to the membrane; the probe seeks out the fragments that have polymorphic DNA segments and attaches to them. (Initially, two types of probes were used in forensic DNA testing: the multi-locus probe, which focused on several loci, or locations, within several chromosomes; and the single-locus probe, which focused on one region within one chromosome. American law enforcement, as well as most public and private labs, currently use the single-locus probe.) Because the probes are radioactive, when an X-ray photograph—called an autoradiograph—is taken, the pieces that the DNA have attached to appear as dark patches. Most labs try to get results from a minimum of four probes. The X-ray photograph, now known as a DNA print, looks somewhat like the bar code used for scanning at the grocery store.
- The DNA print is then compared with the DNA evidence print processed from the crime scene.

If the prints match, the odds are extremely high that the samples came from the same person (assuming that the lab conducted the tests properly). In early DNA cases, experts sometimes estimated the odds of two matching samples *not* coming from the same person at many billions to one. This was often an overstatement based on the failure to take into account a crucial fact: because genes are inherited, genetic markers—the polymorphisms that DNA fingerprinting utilizes—occur with varying frequencies in different populations. If, to use an obvious example, a DNA sample were obtained from a member of a remote tribe in the Amazon rain forest, the odds of getting a matching DNA fingerprint by testing a random person from anywhere in the world might indeed be many billions to one. But the odds would go down considerably—to perhaps 10 million to one—if the second sample were taken from a member of the same tribe in the Amazon. Those are still really long odds, but the reason there is even that much of a chance is that DNA fingerprinting tests only a small portion of a person's genetic code. Testing the entire genetic code would eliminate virtually all chance of a false match, but with current technology that is not feasible.

DNA testing, which was used in a criminal trial for the first time in England in 1987, quickly became a favored tool of law enforcement and prosecutors in the United States. Sometimes the technology astonishes laypersons—and unwary criminals. For example, DNA evidence helped convict a suspect in the World Trade Center bombing of 1993. The suspect had mailed a letter to the *New York Times* claiming credit for the attack in the name of a group called the Fifth Liberation Brigade. The FBI's DNA Unit obtained a DNA fingerprint from the saliva used to seal the envelope.

DNA testing has also been used to *clear* some 2,000 suspects in the United States since 1988. One such suspect was Derrick Coleman, at the time a star basketball player for the New Jersey Nets, who was accused of raping a woman in a Detroit hotel room on July 15, 1994. Authorities dropped all charges against Coleman after DNA analysis of semen samples taken during the rape investigation failed to match the basketball player's DNA profile.

Advantages and disadvantages of DNA testing

Advantages:

- **Accuracy:** The chance of finding two people (excluding identical twins) with the same DNA profile is currently estimated at between 100 million to one and 30 billion to one.
- **Durability:** Under ideal conditions DNA lasts for thousands of years, so it can be used in old criminal cases. DNA testing can be done even when there are only skeletal remains.
- **Versatility:** Any biological material can be submitted for DNA testing, and DNA tests can prove innocence as well as guilt. DNA testing is particularly useful in forcible rape cases because it can provide positive individual identification from a semen sample. DNA profiling is also useful in investigations of similar crimes because it can prove or disprove that a single perpetrator is responsible.
- **Potential for other applications:** A military DNA database would mean that there might never be another "unknown soldier." DNA identification could also aid in the location of missing children. After the human genome is entirely mapped, a DNA sample left at a crime scene could tell investigators such things as the subject's race, eye and hair color, and physical build.

Disadvantages:

- **Cost:** DNA tests are 50 to 100 times more expensive than traditional serology testing.
- **Time:** Since most of the tests are done in special or private labs, specimens must be shipped and take a long time to process.
- **Admissibility:** Currently all states accept DNA tests, but different states have different laws regarding how results can be used in court. That, combined with the judge's discretion on expert testimony, can make jury results vary.
- **Complexity:** DNA testing is a complex and delicate process, requiring considerable expertise in order to ensure accuracy and the certitude needed for jurisprudence. That complexity can make juries confused about the significance and reliability of DNA results. And because there are different ways of estimating population frequency data, widely varying claims about the odds of DNA matches can cause further confusion.
- **Lack of standards:** There are no national standards for forensic DNA tests.

DNA fingerprinting has also been used to exonerate people convicted before the technology came into use, including at least 10 death-row inmates. Edward Honaker, a 44-year-old welder, was sentenced to three life terms plus 34 years for the kidnapping and rape of a 19-year-old woman. During the 1984 trial, Honaker's lawyers argued that the semen found on the victim's body, which contained sperm cells, couldn't have come from the defendant because he had had a vasectomy. They speculated that the sample had actually come from the woman's boyfriend. Nevertheless, the jury believed the testimony of the woman and her boyfriend that Honaker had kidnapped her at gunpoint, driven her to a remote mountain cabin in Virginia, and repeatedly raped her. After serving 10 years in prison, Honaker won an appeal to have DNA tests run on the 10-year-old semen sample, the victim's boyfriend, and himself. The results showed that the semen had not come from either Honaker or the boyfriend, and Honaker was released.

●   ●   ●

Just as DNA testing has revolutionized the use of biological materials in the investigation of crime, another piece of equipment, the *mass spectrometer*, has revolutionized forensic chemistry and toxicology. Researchers estimate that there are about 10 million organic chemicals. And because each of these 10 million could be combined with one or more other chemicals, an almost infinite number of mixtures is possible. The mass spectrometer, initially developed for use in the petrochemical and pharmaceutical industries, allows the scientist-technician to identify the chemical composition of a sample by providing molecular "fingerprints" of all its constituents. The results are compared with known fingerprints of other chemicals. In the past, chemical analysis was limited to what could be examined under a microscope. With the mass

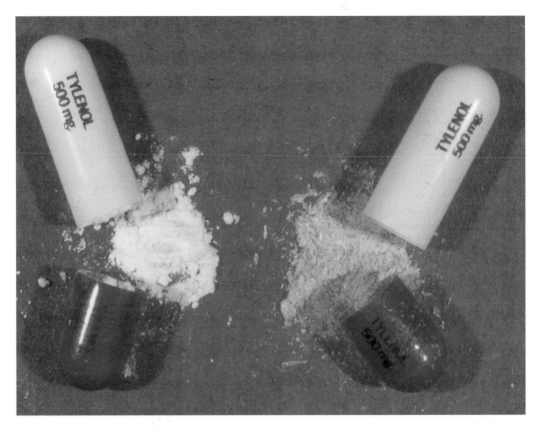

A normal Tylenol capsule (left) alongside a poison-filled capsule. In 1982 an anonymous killer tampered with Tylenol packages, replacing the pain-relief compound with potassium cyanide. Seven people in the Chicago area died before the product was pulled from store shelves and the chief of the FBI's Chemical Unit devised a way to scan Tylenol packages for the presence of cyanide.

spectrometer, scientists can identify the presence of a specific drug or chemical in extremely minute quantities—say, 100 nanograms (a nanogram is one-billionth of a gram).

A previous chapter described the importance of collecting small particles, such as fiber evidence. Remember that the main characteristics of the fiber evidence are put to the test in order to make comparisons. First, the general type and generic classifications are determined, along with all the other physical clues like coarseness, machine marks made during processing, shape, the presence of artificial fibers, and of course, the color. In a chemical laboratory, a color—even a primary color—is never pure. A hue or color is created on fabrics by mixing various dyes. And while the colors cannot be discerned by simple visual examination, an instrument called the *microspectrophotometer* basically produces a "spectral fingerprint" of the color. When different dye analysis shows two color fingerprints as being identical, it is very strong evidence for proving that two fibers found in different places are from the same source.

In 1982 seven people died in Chicago after taking Tylenol capsules that had been laced with potassium cyanide. Recognition dawned on authorities and the shocked public that a new type of crime, product tampering, had emerged. With the extent of the tampering unknown, merchants immediately pulled Tylenol from their shelves.

Investigators needed to determine how many packages had been poisoned, but short of checking every package by hand, a logistical nightmare, how could this be done? The FBI gave the task a high priority.

The chief of the bureau's Chemical Unit, Roger Martz, believed the answer lay in basic chemistry. Since potassium absorbs X rays, he reasoned, a chemical like potassium cyanide would show up on an X ray, while the main ingredient in Tylenol, acetaminophen, would not. After examining thousands of packages using a screening process similar to the process used to screen luggage at airports, the investigators found several other tainted samples. Unfortunately, the perpetrator was never caught.

Another helpful machine, called a *spectograph*, turns speech sounds into identifiable measured electronic impulses of the voice. Spectograph results are used for comparison, and although they have sometimes been admitted as evidence in court, they are not always accepted at trials. Many people believe they are unreliable for voice recognition.

Every person's voice is different. But voice qualities may change from one day to the next. Since a single word or even a sound requires effort from our vocal cords, palate, tongue, teeth, and lips, an illness, a change in air quality, or even psychological stress can change the sound. Thus far, even industrial equipment that relies on voice activation must be reintroduced to its commanding voice each day.

One case that did hinge on a voiceprint, though, involved a Texas convenience store robbery and murder. Police arrested a suspect who looked like the man on the store's surveillance tape. Luckily for him, after a voiceprint expert compared his voice with the tones captured on the audio portion of the tape, the expert determined that the suspect was *not* the person who had killed the clerk.

♣   ♣   ♣

The *polygraph machine*, also known as the *lie detector*, has a long history and is still used today. It is, however, much misunderstood by the general public. Basically, the polygraph uses mechanical and electronic instrumentation to measure, and graphically record, three physiological indicators that, in most people, change under the stress of telling a lie. As the polygraph examiner asks the subject a series of carefully controlled yes-or-no questions, the subject's rate and depth of respiration are measured by straps fixed around the abdomen and chest; cardiovascular activity is measured by a blood-pressure cuff strapped around the biceps; and electrodermal response, an indication of perspiration, is measured by electrodes placed on the fingertips. The initial questions, such as the subject's name, are routine. They are designed to establish a baseline against which responses to later questions can be compared.

While polygraph results themselves cannot be used in court unless an agreement and stipulation of counsel

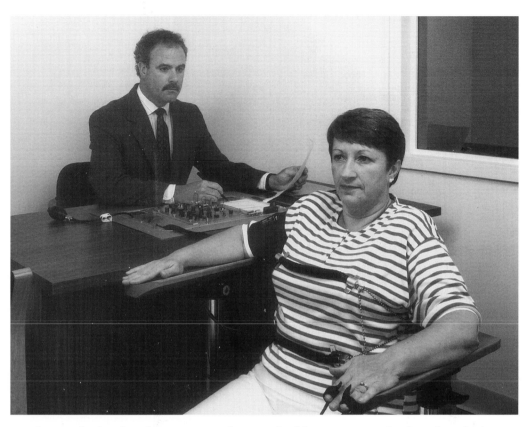

is obtained, the lie detector can be a valuable investigative tool when administered by a trained polygraphist. It can verify known or expected information, help in the development of leads, or point toward the need for additional evidence collection.

Unfortunately, though, the polygraph isn't foolproof. Even ordinary people have been known to beat the machine, reportedly by using techniques such as changing their sleep patterns or taking caffeine before the test. In addition, habitual liars can pass because lying isn't stressful for them. And many sociopaths have the capacity to mentally separate their "good" and "bad" selves. They attribute their crimes to the other, bad self, while the good self stays in control during the polygraph examination.

A polygraph, or lie-detector, test. As the woman answers a series of controlled questions asked by the trained examiner, the machine will monitor her respiration, blood pressure, and electrodermal response (a measure of perspiration)—three physiological indicators that in most people change under the stress of lying.

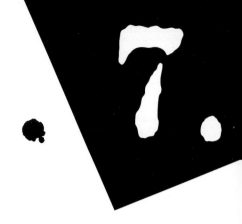

BEHAVIORAL PROFILING

Jeffrey Dahmer is led into court for arraignment. Dahmer's polite, mild-mannered exterior masked a monster within: he murdered at least 17 boys and young men, cut up their bodies, and in some cases ate their flesh. While most of us recoil at the mere thought of such gruesome deeds, behavioral profilers study every detail of a heinous crime in order to get inside the mind of the criminal who committed it. Their insights can help police catch the offender.

There's a wonderful, naive quote in the 1956 science-fiction film *Forbidden Planet*. As two men prepare to enter a private dwelling occupied by a demented inventor and his daughter—with the express purpose of finding evidence of malice—the commander, played by Leslie Nielsen, turns to his somewhat reluctant comrade and says, "We're all part monsters in our subconscious; that's why we have laws and religion."

To today's audiences, the movie may seem hopelessly old-fashioned, but the scriptwriter was right on the mark about one thing. We are, all of us, part monsters in our subconscious. And that is as true now as it was in 1956—or in 1856 or 856, for that matter. Efforts to understand the complexities of the human psyche, and especially to make sense of evil, have spawned various ideas throughout history. Since ancient times some people have held the belief that the universe as a whole, or human beings specifically, have a dual nature, a good and an evil side. Humans' propensity for thinking about and doing evil has often been called "the dark side."

In the modern world examples of a particularly frightening sort of evildoer—the serial killer—aren't terribly hard to find. In general, though, modern society tends to deny the existence of a dark side, preferring instead to explain the most heinous acts as the work of people whose individual psychopathologies set them completely apart from the rest of us. The killer is seen as an aberration, a monster, not as someone who gave vent to impulses that all of us might have deep within. On a certain level we expect the killer to look like a monster as well, to be immediately and readily distinguishable from the rest of us. People are continually surprised, it seems, when a person who has lived among them—a person like the harmless-looking Jeffrey Dahmer—turns out to be a butcher and a cannibal. It's almost a convention for neighbors to exclaim to news reporters, "He was such a nice, quiet boy! Who would have thought?"

Who would have thought indeed. In fact, there are people whose job it is to think about the mentality and motivations of society's most horrifying criminals. These men and women bump up against the very darkest side of the human mind every day. Called "criminalists" or "behavioral profilers," they know intimately the signs and patterns associated with criminal behavior. And by combining this general knowledge with a careful examination of the specific crime's characteristics, they can tell police what kind of person to look for—and in some cases, how to catch him. This technique of getting at the psychological makeup of the criminal from an analysis of the crime is known as *criminal profiling* or *behavioral profiling*.

The history of criminal profiling may have begun in the mind of a writer. In three short stories written in the 1840s, Edgar Allan Poe introduced readers to C. Auguste Dupin, a French amateur detective who says his plans include a way for the detective to "seduce into error or hurry into miscalculation" the killer.

A century later, between 1940 and 1957, with a temporary suspension during World War II, real-life New York City was terrorized by an unknown subject dubbed "the Mad Bomber." During this period, the bomber planted more than 30 explosive packages at various places around the city, including Radio City Music Hall and Grand Central Station. After the bombings he taunted the police in letters sent to newspapers. Investigators were stymied by the case until they requested the services of Dr. James Brussel, a New York City psychiatrist.

Brussel carefully examined the evidence and came up with a psychological profile. The Mad Bomber would, he predicted, be a paranoid middle-aged man who obsessively loved his mother while deeply hating his father. But Brussel didn't confine his profile to strictly psychological matters. He also told police their man would be single and residing with a brother or sister in Connecticut; foreign-born, probably from eastern Europe; Roman Catholic; neat; and heavy. He even predicted that the bomber, when arrested, would be wearing a buttoned, double-breasted suit. When police finally arrested George Metesky in Waterbury, Connecticut, in 1957, they discovered that almost all of what Brussel predicted about the Mad Bomber was correct—down to the buttoned, double-breasted suit.

For his remarkable feat of psychological profiling, Brussel soon bore the nickname "the Sherlock Holmes of the Couch." But while his profile seemed, at the time, almost magical, Brussel's technique wasn't all that mysterious. As a psychiatrist, he explained, he was used to predicting what a patient might do in a given situation, knowing the patient's psychological makeup. For his profile, he had simply worked in reverse, predicting what the subject was like from what he had done. Insights from his knowledge of psychiatry had been

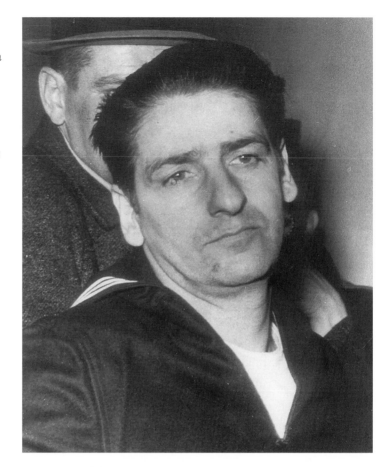

Albert DeSalvo, the Boston Strangler, who raped and murdered at least 13 women in the early 1960s. Behavioral profiling fell into disrepute after a committee of distinguished psychiatrists and psychologists that had been convened to help police in the Boston Strangler case came up with a wildly inaccurate profile of the killer.

indispensable, of course, but so had a careful analysis of linguistic clues in the letters, a bit of intuition, and logic.

A few years later, Brussel's experience and judgment were again put to the test when he was asked to join a committee of experts working on the Boston Strangler case. The strangler raped and killed at least 13 women between 1962 and 1964. The committee members, distinguished psychologists and psychiatrists, predicted that there were actually *two* murderers: one, a loner who worked as a schoolteacher; the other, a homosexual with an intense hatred of women. Brussel didn't agree with his colleagues' conclusions, but when the killings mysteriously stopped, the committee disbanded.

The reason the killings had stopped, it later became clear, was that police had arrested the murderer for another crime, breaking and entering. After being sent to a mental institution, Albert DeSalvo confessed to the Boston Strangler murders, revealing details about the crimes only the killer would know. The profiles the committee had drawn up turned out to be way off the mark. There weren't two killers. DeSalvo wasn't a loner, a schoolteacher, or a homosexual who hated women. He was actually a handyman, married with children.

Although the profile Brussel had given the police fit the actual killer much better, the Boston Strangler case made the law enforcement community as a whole skeptical of the merits of criminal profiling. Several FBI agents produced occasional, and somewhat informal, profiles upon request from local police, but years would pass before the technique again won widespread acceptance.

A key test emerged in 1973, with the abduction of a seven-year-old girl from a campground in Montana. When an agent from the FBI's office in Bozeman referred the case to the FBI's Behavioral Science Unit, the resulting profile described a young, white male (as statistics in such cases predicted) living in the vicinity of the victim's campsite. Voyeuristic and homicidal (though no body had been found, the profilers believed the girl had been murdered), he was an organized type—that is, he planned the crime, bringing with him and taking away whatever weapons or tools he needed. He was a loner of average or higher intelligence, another statistical prediction. The profile fit a suspect in the case. But no concrete evidence linked that suspect, 23-year-old Vietnam veteran David Meierhofer, to the crime.

The following year, a female acquaintance of Meierhofer's disappeared, and suspicion again fell on him. Meierhofer volunteered to take a lie-detector test and a so-called truth-serum examination, both of which he passed. Normally, that would have been sufficient to clear him. But the FBI's profilers predicted that the killer could pass such tests, and they urged the authorities not to drop Meierhofer as a suspect. The profilers also felt that Meierhofer might contact his victim's parents to relive the excitement of the crime. He did, and authorities taped the call. Analysis of the taped conversation led one FBI profiler to conclude that Meierhofer would be susceptible to pressure by women, so the victim's mother confronted him face-to-face. Guilt-ridden, Meierhofer later made another call to the victim's mother that provided enough evidence to obtain a search warrant for his apartment. There police found body parts from the victim, and Meierhofer was arrested. Without the aid of the psychological profile, it is unlikely that the crime would have been solved.

Soon after the Meierhofer case, New York City police turned to forensic psychiatry and psychology for assistance in a high-profile serial murder investigation. Over a period of 13 months, from 1976 to 1977, a killer shot female victims and couples, often as they sat in parked cars. He left notes to police at some of the crime scenes, and he also mailed many letters to newspapers. From a phrase in one of these letters the killer acquired the name "Son of Sam." Dr. Murray S. Miron, a professor at Syracuse University, performed a psycholinguistic analysis of Son of Sam's communications. The profile Miron developed closely fit the man arrested for the murders, David Berkowitz.

Although professional investigators were beginning to realize that psychiatrists and psychologists could be a great aid in certain criminal investigations, the use of profiles remained sporadic until 1978. That year the FBI established the Psychological Profiling Program within the Behavioral Science Unit at the FBI Academy in Quantico, Virginia. The bureau began by compiling a library of known cases.

An initiative that would have profound implications for the future of behavioral profiling also began in the late 1970s when FBI profiler Robert Ressler and his associates began interviewing convicted serial killers and rapists about their lives and their crimes. In the past, profiling had relied almost exclusively on the profiler's own experience and intuition. But Ressler's program, called the Criminal Personality Research Project (CPRP), began systematizing knowledge in the field. Interviewing the offenders gave profilers a glimpse not only at the *whys* of their crimes but also at the *hows*—how they found and subdued their victims, how they avoided detection. The CPRP also added immensely to knowledge about the various types of serial offenders, and to the patterns of behavior that characterized each type. And, as Ressler revealed in his 1992 book *Whoever Fights Monsters*, it confirmed the existence of certain criminal behaviors that had long been postulated by police officers and criminologists—for example, returning to the scene of the crime. All of this made profiling a much more systematic and fact-based endeavor.

Despite some public misperceptions, however, profilers don't actually catch criminals or even point police to the one person who could have committed a particular crime or series of crimes. "The real task," Robert Ressler explains in *Whoever Fights Monsters*,

> is to whittle down the universe of potential suspects, to eliminate the least likely ones and allow the on-site investigators to focus on realistic targets. Thus, if we are able to say with a high degree of probable accuracy that the suspect in a crime is a male, we've eliminated about 50 percent of the population who are not males. The category "adult males" is a smaller fraction of the population; "single white males," an even smaller number. . . . Every added category makes the band of possible suspects slimmer—for instance, we might suggest that the likely criminal is unemployed, or one who has previously received treatment for mental disease, or that it is a person who lives within walking distance of the crime scene.

In his book *Mindhunter,* former FBI agent John Douglas adds that profilers can perform two other important functions. First, they can suggest proactive techniques that police might use during an investigation to draw the criminal out. For example, they might suggest that a memorial service be held for a victim because the killer is likely to attend. Second, after a suspect has been apprehended, profilers can suggest the best method of police interrogation, and they can also tell prosecutors how to bring out the defendant's true personality at trial.

Criminal profiling is best used as an investigative tool after other, more traditional methods have been explored. It is usually employed in serial murder cases and in investigations of any especially heinous crime in which some form of psychopathology is evident, including sadistic torture in sexual assaults, evisceration, postmortem mutilation, motiveless fire setting, and ritualistic murder.

Today, police from jurisdictions across the country enlist the aid of the FBI's behavioral profilers, the acknowledged experts in the field, when they are confronted with cases such as the above. The bureau's profiling technique, called the Criminal Investigative Analysis Program (CIAP), has gained a reputation for accurately describing the perpetrators of these kinds of violent crimes.

Various elements go into the creation of a good behavioral profile. First, there is careful analysis of the crime scene. In this respect, profiling begins at the same point as any forensic investigation—with questions: What happened here? What did the perpetrator do to subdue the victim? How did the victim respond?

Next, there is the crime itself. "To know the offender," John Douglas has declared, "look at the crime." One of the basic tenets of profiling is that a serial killer (or any other offender whose crimes stem from an aberrant personality), no matter how intelligent or careful,

cannot conceal his own psychopathology. A skilled profiler will be able to read it from the crimes themselves. The reason: unlike more-typical offenders, for whom crime is a means to an end (for example, getting money), serial murderers see the killing itself as the end. It represents the fulfillment of their violent fantasies, and for the act to be emotionally satisfying, they must do it in a certain manner. The profiler can see the patterns of pathological behavior in individual acts.

The profiler also uses statistical predictions to flesh out the portrait of the offender revealed by the crime scene and the crime. For example, most serial murderers are between the ages of 25 and 35. Almost all are men. If the killer isn't psychotic (severely mentally ill

The werewolves and vampires of horror tales may have originated as efforts to explain the deeds of actual serial or sex killers. Here: a scene from the 1922 German vampire film Nosferatu.

Phrenology, a pseudoscience popular in the 19th century, attempted to link mental capacities and character with skull shape.

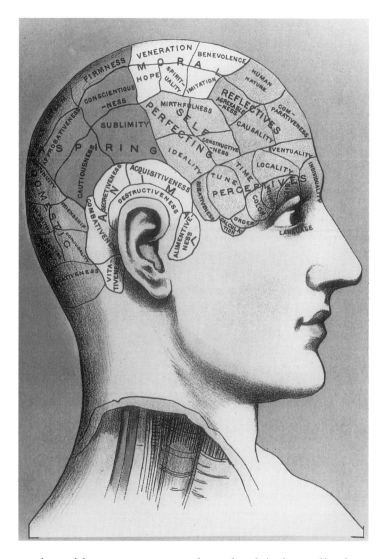

and unable to perceive reality clearly), he will often have had a childhood history of cruelty to animals or fire starting, and some stressful event (such as the loss of a job or the end of a relationship) will have immediately preceded the first killing. If the killer is psychotic (something that is usually apparent from the crime), he will probably have been institutionalized before. All of these predictions are based on the known characteristics of serial murderers.

Like other forensic sciences, profiling is a puzzle. The solution comes from a combination of knowledge, experience, logic, and insight. As Robert Ressler says, "What plus why equals who."

Such an equation may succinctly explain the profiler's work, but it cannot answer society's first question: How can people do such unspeakably horrible things to other people? That is a question that defies easy answers.

People who torture and kill others in monstrous fashion may always have existed, and fanciful stories may have been earlier societies' efforts to deal with what they could not understand. The ancient Sumerians believed that behind the seven gates in the otherworld resided the Old Ones, the Gods of Evil, who stood in wait for a time when they could pass through the gates and take over the world. Tales of werewolves, people transformed into wolves who killed and mutilated other people on full-moon nights, exist in many societies. They, like the also-common vampire tales, may have originated with actual mutilation murders. Today, behavior described in the horror tales of earlier societies is known to exist and has been given names such as *haematodipsia* (a sexual compulsion to taste human blood), *necrophilia* (sexual stimulation from seeing and touching a corpse), and *necrophagy* (a desire to eat the flesh of the dead).

As humanity's worldview changed under the influence of science, tales of evil gods, werewolves, and vampires were replaced with efforts to explain deviant behavior more scientifically. The results, of course, didn't always reflect reality all that accurately. For example, the "science" of *phrenology*, which enjoyed substantial popularity throughout most of the 19th century, claimed to predict character and temperament through analysis of skull shape.

The rise of psychology and psychiatry opened up more-promising avenues. Sigmund Freud, for example,

Dr. Kathryn Ednie, a forensic psychiatrist, testifies at a 1998 murder trial. Making science understandable for the courts is a vital function of specialists from all forensic disciplines.

linked much human behavior with unresolved sexual conflicts. He also believed that humans possess a "death instinct," the drawback of a modern civilization filled to overflowing with frustration.

Today, experts view serial murder as a sexually motivated offense, regardless of whether victims are actually raped or sexually abused. A percentage of serial murderers are psychotic, and their behavior can be attributed to their mental illness. Most, however, are considered psychopaths—they perceive reality clearly but feel no social or moral obligations. Childhood abuse figures in the backgrounds of most, but such abuse doesn't sufficiently explain their behavior, as most people who are abused don't go on to become serial killers.

Some research has pointed to organic factors, such as an additional male Y chromosome or abnormal levels of the neurochemicals serotonin and norepinephrine, in predisposing individuals to impulsive aggression, premeditated cruelty, or excessive violence. But not everyone accepts these genetically based causes. It may be that an interaction of genetic and environmental factors produces the most flagrant kinds of deviancy.

What is accepted—and what ensures the continued importance of behavioral profilers—is that the number of documented serial murderers has risen alarmingly in modern times. In the book *Malicious Intent*, author Sean Mactire writes that "prior to 1888, only a dozen men, women or unknown suspects committed the kind of horrific crime that would earn them a place in the annals of criminal history. However, from 1889 on, almost a year hasn't gone by without one or more serial killers or other kind of terribly vicious, violent criminals being caught and tried somewhere in America, Canada or Europe."

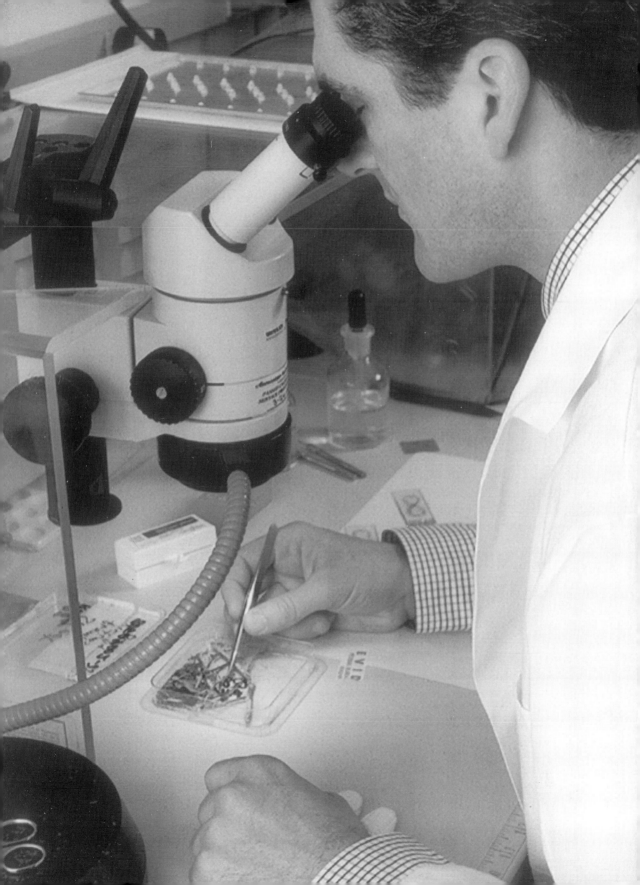

The Future of Forensic Science

We've come a long way since the fictional Sherlock Holmes analyzed cigar ash, boot soil, and a man's fingernails for evidence of malice and misdeed. As technology becomes ever more sophisticated, the potential role of forensic science also expands. But what is technically possible and what is actually done are two different matters. As a practical matter, forensic science is limited by the budgetary resources it is allocated and by the ability of law enforcement and criminal justice professionals to understand the significance of new technologies. In a real sense, forensic science simply responds to the needs of the law enforcement and criminal justice systems it serves.

Drug testing is a good example of how changing justice priorities have influenced forensic science. Historically, drug testing in the criminal justice system has been pretty much synonymous with *urinalysis*, the chemical analysis of urine samples. (Urine contains

A forensic scientist performing hair analysis. Hair is used in drug testing, a major priority of the criminal justice system and the source of a large portion of forensic laboratories' current caseloads.

metabolites, waste products from the body's metabolic system, including the metabolites of drugs.) But, as Professor Tom Mieczkowski says in an article for the *National Institute of Justice Journal,* "as drug testing as a fairly routine procedure enters its third decade, the assumptions may no longer reflect reality because the types of drugs attracting the most interest are changing, and the technology to detect them is evolving to meet new needs."

Over the years, several advances in technology have made urinalysis more efficient and effective. Chromatography, a system whereby molecules of different substances can be separated one from the other and identified by reading their characteristic patterns and bandings, is sometimes employed. This technique, first used in the 1960s, soon developed into the more sensitive thin-layer chromatography (TLC), but the procedure was still slow and expensive. Two further advances, high-performance liquid chromatography and gas-liquid chromatography, yielded improved accuracy but did not measurably address the issues of speed and cost.

During the 1970s, a major technological development occurred with the *immunoassay* procedure. This technique uses antigen-antibody reaction. For example, if someone's urine were being checked for the presence of methadone, methadone antibodies would be added to the urine. Any methadone drug present would immediately combine with these antibodies. After the addition of enzyme-labeled methadone drug, the quantity of the uncombined drug that is left is then measured. An important advance over TLC, this procedure was more specific and quite reliable for screening. In addition, it lowered costs and decreased the time required to achieve results because it became mechanized, allowing for large-scale processing.

In the late 1980s, recognizing the link between drug abuse and crime, criminal justice professionals began to come to a general consensus that persons who abstain from drug use are better prospects for probation. This was a major development in thinking. By 1989, the newly established Office of National Drug Control Policy recommended "comprehensive use" of drug testing for virtually all categories of people in the criminal justice system. This new mandate has created a great demand for even faster and cheaper drug testing because of the vastly increased frequency of testing.

New technologies are emerging to address these needs. These methods are more cost-effective and less intrusive than urinalysis. Most important, perhaps, because they may be able to detect newly discovered illicit drugs, they can help the criminal justice system keep pace with changing patterns of drug abuse. One such technology is hair analysis, which has been suggested as a supplement to urine testing. When introduced into court as evidence, the results of hair analysis have generally been upheld. Saliva testing has been used to identify cocaine and cannabinoids (such as marijuana), but its full potential has still to be realized.

Another new concept is the use of sweat patches. Like urine, sweat, one of the body's ways of eliminating waste, contains drugs and drug metabolites and can be analyzed with technologies similar to those used in urinalysis. The adhesive patch, which is worn for extended periods to allow for the accumulation of sufficient quantities of sweat, provides a long "window of detection." A similar technology, the "smart patch," is pushing the envelope of research. Unlike the standard patch, it produces results instantly with embedded microelectronic chips. Not only can the smart patch date when the drugs were administered, but it can also indicate their level of concentration. Though they appear to hold great promise, smart patches have yet to be extensively field-tested.

The evolution of drug-testing technology shows the influence of factors such as changing levels and types of drug use, awareness of the problem, and the political response. Researchers note, however, that the technological advances spurred by these factors appear at times to have outstripped some agencies' capacities to effectively use the information generated.

And that brings us to another technology that has gradually become an established part of the criminal justice system: DNA testing. Despite early controversies and challenges by defense attorneys, DNA test results are now routinely admitted in the courtroom. In "The Unrealized Potential of DNA Testing," Victor Walter Weedn and John W. Hicks reveal that more than 200 published court opinions support this use, and in 1996 "there were more than 17,000 cases involving forensic DNA in this country alone."

Why has the justice system come to embrace this technology? First, DNA can withstand harsh environmental insults; second, it is likely to be detectable for many years in bone or body fluid stains from older criminal cases; and third, virtually all biological evidence found at crime scenes can be subjected to DNA testing. Again, however, efforts to use DNA have fallen short of the potential because much of what can be used for testing—fingernail scrapings, saliva from cigarettes and chewing gum, hair, skin cells, and a host of other biological specimens—are not recovered from crime scenes. Other limitations involve a lack of sufficient laboratory funding, the time-consuming methods of testing, an inability to test in the field, and the challenge of automating DNA evidence databases.

But recent developments tell us that some of these downsides are already being dealt with. In October 1998, the Combined DNA Index System, an FBI database, went on-line. At the time, the database contained the genetic fingerprints of 250,000 convicted felons from all 50 states, along with more than 4,500 DNA samples from unsolved crimes. Accessible by police departments around the country, the database could

prove to be of enormous importance in helping to solve past and future crimes. As Dawn Herkenham, chief of the FBI's Forensic Sciences Unit, says, "A criminal can change his residence but he can't change his DNA. Now a state can upload its own [DNA] crime scene samples and make a hit, literally from coast to coast."

Convicted kidnapper Norman Jimmerson might have gotten paroled and slipped away from the system if it hadn't been for the DNA sample recovered from a long-unsolved rape case in Williamsburg, Virginia. Although the state of Virginia drew Jimmerson's blood in 1991, it took four years for the DNA to be analyzed and made available to authorities because of the backlog in Virginia's crime lab.

FBI officials Donald Kerr (left) and Dwight Adams announce the opening of the National DNA Index System, October 13, 1998. The DNA database enables police officers from around the country to compare the genetic fingerprints of convicted felons with evidence they've gathered in their own investigations.

That brings us to a core problem: in the nation's government crime labs, there exists a total backlog of more than 300,000 DNA samples taken from convicts. Attorney General Janet Reno convened a panel to study this problem, and a controversial solution was considered: hiring private labs to analyze the DNA samples. It's estimated that a single private lab could eliminate the backlog in 12 to 18 months at a total cost of only $15 million, or $50 per sample. Critics of this solution, however, worry that turning over personal genetic material to the private sector could lead to exploitation. For example, they claim that because a DNA profile can reveal the likelihood that the subject will develop certain diseases, information could be used by potential insurers or employers to deny insurance coverage or employment to offenders. Proponents of privatizing DNA sample analysis counter that legitimate privacy concerns could be accommodated if samples were identified by a code number. As of this writing, the resolution of the issue remains in doubt.

The potential use of private labs also leads to perhaps the most important issue in forensic science today: personnel and training. Dr. Werner Spitz, former chief medical examiner of Detroit, asks, "Is it [death investigation in the United States] an enlightened system? No, it's not. It's really no better than what they have in many Third World countries."

Unfortunately, death investigation in the United States has been operating under a hodgepodge of methodological and performance standards. According to the new *National Guidelines for Death Investigation* manual written by the U.S. Department of Justice:

> There is no 'system' of death investigation that covers more than 3,000 jurisdictions in the country. No nationally accepted guidelines or standards of practice exist for individuals responsible for performing death-scene investigations. No professional degree, license, certification, or minimum educational requirements exist, nor is there a

commonly accepted training curriculum. Not even a common job title exists for the thousands of people who routinely perform death investigations in this country.

In an effort to address those pressing problems, the highly experienced professionals who served on the National Medicolegal Review Panel issued guidelines for nationwide standards. But the adoption of these guidelines, which depends on voluntary action by each individual jurisdiction or by the passage of bills in state legislatures, remains in doubt.

In addition to the need for standard practices and technical know-how, today's criminalists must, as the famous forensic science author and consultant Richard Saferstein says, "discover and master the role of the expert witness. A good courtroom demeanor and the ability to communicate thoughts and ideas in clear, concise terms are absolutely essential if the scientist's examination and conclusions are to be properly and effectively presented at a hearing or in court." For what good is technology married with evidence if it serves only to confuse jurors and muddle their decisions? Next to observance of a person's constitutional rights, the ability of juries to understand the evidence is per-haps the most crucial factor in obtaining justice. And that is what the end result of any forensic science inves-tigation should be: the correct and honest application of scientific evidence.

Research conducted for the National Institute of Justice tells us some important things about the state of forensic testing and evidence today, as well as what is needed for the future. In a survey focusing on six diverse jurisdictions and using random samplings and a series of interviews, the researchers observed that only about a quarter of crime laboratory caseloads involve personal or property crimes. Two-thirds of the work is for the identification of drugs and narcotics and the determination of the blood alcohol levels of suspected drunk drivers. What this means is that most forensic

A New Hampshire State Police officer works inside the state's Major Crimes Unit van, which is driven to crime scenes for forensic evidence gathering. Such forward-looking programs demonstrate a recognition of the importance of forensic science in crime investigation, but fulfilling the vast potential of the field will require the allocation of greater resources.

laboratories are bogged down in drug caseloads and have a difficult time responding to other investigations.

The study showed that drugs and fingerprints make up between 60 and 80 percent of the evidence described in various laboratory reports. Also, laboratories tend to focus on evidence needed for mandatory prosecution or on cases in which evidence is needed to decisively link the defendant with the crime.

The next most highly used forensic evidence was reported for firearms, blood and bloodstains, and semen, even though usage in these categories actually dropped during the period studied. Researchers believe the reason for this decline is that investigators have less time for additional cases because of the time spent with increasingly sophisticated tests and the emphasis on quality assurance.

Of the more than 300 crime laboratories in the United States, 80 percent are located *within* police agencies. Even though crime labs are used largely by the courts and meet the jurisdiction's prosecutorial needs, the labs themselves are funded by the police. Most, in fact, are chronically underfunded. Reports indicate that on average, crime labs account for less than one-half of one percent of police budgets.

In order to ensure the future contributions of forensic science, funding issues must be addressed. And funding is related to the perceptions of what might be called forensic science's primary constituency: prosecutors. If prosecutors can be made to see the potential importance of forensic science in a variety of cases— and to use forensic testing routinely—pressure would be created for increased funding. Advocates for forensic science must take the lead in educating prosecutors.

One positive force for the nation's forensic laboratories is a new billion-dollar boost from the government. Starting in the fall of 1999, state and local crime labs will be able to tap into a federal grant program providing more than $1.25 billion over five years—money designed to help labs facing staff shortages and the growing demand for their services. Senator Mike DeWine of Ohio, a sponsor of the Crime Identification Technology Act, says, "What labs do is integral to solving crimes. This bill says loud and clear that they should not be forgotten."

Sherlock Holmes would surely agree with that.

Bibliography

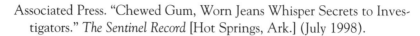

Associated Press. "Chewed Gum, Worn Jeans Whisper Secrets to Investigators." *The Sentinel Record* [Hot Springs, Ark.] (July 1998).

De Forest, Peter R.; Henry C. Lee; and R. E. Gaensslen. *Forensic Science: An Introduction to Criminalistics*. New York: McGraw-Hill, 1983.

Douglas, John, and Mark Olshaker. *Mindhunter: Inside the FBI's Elite Serial Crime Unit*. New York: Scribner, 1995.

Evans, Colin. *The Casebook of Forensic Detection: How Science Solved 100 of the World's Most Baffling Crimes*. New York: John Wiley & Sons, 1996.

Feldman, Philip M. *Criminal Behavior: A Psychological Analysis*. New York: John Wiley & Sons, 1978.

Fisher, David. *Hard Evidence: How Detectives Inside the FBI's Sci-Crime Lab Have Helped Solve America's Toughest Cases*. New York: Simon & Schuster, 1995.

Gardner, Robert. *Crime Lab 101*. New York: Walker Publishing Co., 1992.

Geberth, Vernon J. *Practical Homicide Investigation: Tactics, Procedures, and Forensic Techniques*. Boca Raton, Fla.: CRC Press, 1996. [Not recommended for laypersons]

HBO. *Dead Men Do Tell Tales* (documentary), broadcast October 12, 1998.

Jones, Charlotte Foltz. *Fingerprints and Talking Bones: How Real-Life Crimes Are Solved*. New York: Delacorte Press, 1997.

Kelly, Delos. *Criminal Behavior: Text and Readings in Criminology*. New York: St. Martin's Press, 1990.

Mactire, Sean. *Malicious Intent: A Writer's Guide to How Murderers, Robbers, Rapists and Other Criminals Think*. Cincinnati, Ohio: Writer's Digest Books, 1995.

Mieczkowski, Tom, and Kim Lersch. "Drug Testing in Criminal Justice: Evolving Uses, Emerging Technologies." *National Institute of Justice Journal* 234 (December 1997): 9–15.

Peterson, Joseph L. *Use of Forensic Evidence by the Police and Courts.* Washington, D.C.: U.S. Department of Justice, National Institute of Justice, 1987: 2, 3, 5.

Ressler, Robert K., and Tom Shachtman. *Whoever Fights Monsters.* New York: St. Martin's Press, 1992.

Saferstein, Richard, Ph.D. *Criminalistics: An Introduction to Forensic Science.* Englewood Cliffs, N.J.: Prentice Hall, 1995.

Territo, Leonard; James B. Halsted; and Max L. Bromley. *Crime & Justice in America: A Human Perspective.* St. Paul, Minn.: West Publishing Co., 1995.

Ubelaker, Douglas H., and Henry Scammell. *Bones: A Forensic Detective's Casebook.* New York: HarperCollins, 1992.

U.S. Department of Justice. *National Guidelines for Death Investigation.* Washington, D.C., NCJ 167568, 1.

Weedn, Victor Walter, and John W. Hicks. "The Unrealized Potential of DNA Testing." *National Institute of Justice Journal* 234 (December 1997): 16–23.

Willing, Richard. "FBI Activates 50-State DNA Database Tuesday." *USA Today* (October 12, 1998): 1.

————. "Plan Would Let Private Labs Do DNA Tests." *USA Today* (October 12, 1998): 1.

Wilson, Keith D., M.D. *Cause of Death: A Writer's Guide to Death, Murder & Forensic Medicine.* Cincinnati, Ohio: Writer's Digest Books, 1992.

Wingate, Anne, Ph.D. *Scene of the Crime: A Writer's Guide to Crime-Scene Investigations.* Cincinnati, Ohio: Writer's Digest Books, 1992.

Zonderman, Jon. *Beyond the Crime Lab: The New Science of Investigation.* New York: John Wiley & Sons, 1990.

Forensic Science Websites

- Forensic Science Resources in a Criminal Fact Investigation Index
  http://www.public.usit.net/rscarp/forensic.htm

- An Introduction to Forensic Firearms Identification
  http://www.geocities.com/~jsdoyle/A_Welcome.htm

- Police Officer's Internet Directory
  http://www.officer.com

- Questioned Document Examination
  http://www.webmasters.net/qde

- Zeno's Forensic Web Page
  http://www.bart.nl/~geradts/forensic.html

Index

Index

Index

ANDREA CAMPBELL, a diplomate with the American College of Forensic Examiners, holds a degree in Criminal Justice and does forensic reconstruction sculpture for law enforcement. She has written several books, articles for a variety of educational magazines, and a weekly newspaper column. She lives in Hot Springs Village, Arkansas, with her husband, Michael.

AUSTIN SARAT is William Nelson Cromwell Professor of Jurisprudence and Political Science at Amherst College, where he also chairs the Department of Law, Jurisprudence and Social Thought. Professor Sarat is the author or editor of 23 books and numerous scholarly articles. Among his books are *Law's Violence, Sitting in Judgment: Sentencing the White Collar Criminal,* and *Justice and Injustice in Law and Legal Theory.* He has received many academic awards and held several prestigious fellowships. He is President of the Law & Society Association and Chair of the Working Group on Law, Culture and the Humanities. In addition, he is a nationally recognized teacher and educator whose teaching has been featured in the *New York Times,* on the *Today* show, and on National Public Radio's *Fresh Air.*

Picture Credits